Escape

A True Story

V. G. Yankovsky

Translated From Russian By
Michael Hintze

This Work Was First Published In Russian In 2001 In The Town Of Vladimir (Russia) As Part Of A Collection Of V.G. Yankovsky's Works Called "Okhota" ("The Hunt').

Editors:

"Zolotye Vorota" ("The Golden Gate") 2001
"Transit X" 2001

Author: V.G. Yankovsky 2001
Russian Edition: Isbn 5- 8257-O257-1
Proof Reader: Eileen M.Hintze
Reviewer: Larissa N. Waterson (Nee Hintze)
Computer Layout: David (Prilezhny) Waterson.

Sydney Australia 2007

Cover Art And Design By George Chernikov

Sarah Louise Snow Stever
Born 6 June 1972, Ann Arbor Michigan
Died 10 November 2007, Atlanta Georgia
Married Kevin Stever, 23 September 2006

Dedication

This first English edition of "Escape: A True Story" is dedicated to my daughter Sarah Louise Snow Stever. Sarah's interest in my family made this book possible. She never stopped researching our origins in Novina, a White Russian settlement which had existed in what is now North Korea.

It was Sarah who discovered the translator in Australia, the author in Russia, and brought them together with myself here in the U.S.

Sarah suddenly passed away at age 35, in the prime of her life, and only 1 year after she had married the man of her dreams. Here is what her husband Kevin Stever wrote for her memorial:

"Sarah was an artist in many ways: hair stylist, writer, singer, and musician. She was the owner and creative spirit of Novina Studio, her salon in Decatur, GA. She loved to explore life and was pursuing her dream of being a screenwriter, poet, and singer-songwriter. She cared deeply about people, treating her clients as friends, and often becoming a part of their lives. She showed her humanity by helping the poor with her church and with many causes related to the kind and humane treatment of animals. Sarah is survived by four very special pets - cats Pasha and Jasper, and dogs Lucy and Sweet Baby Rufus - all of whom she adopted or rescued."

Goodbye for now my gentle warrior, lovely daughter, faithful friend. For you, some verses you liked, by Russell Salamon:

To tell you to sing
is silly,
you have never stopped
singing.
To tell you something you
don't already know is hard
for in your giant laughter
strides open
and the road you carry
you lay before you.

From your laughter
You sow seas and life
And as you sow so shall you
leap.

Elliott Snow February 2008

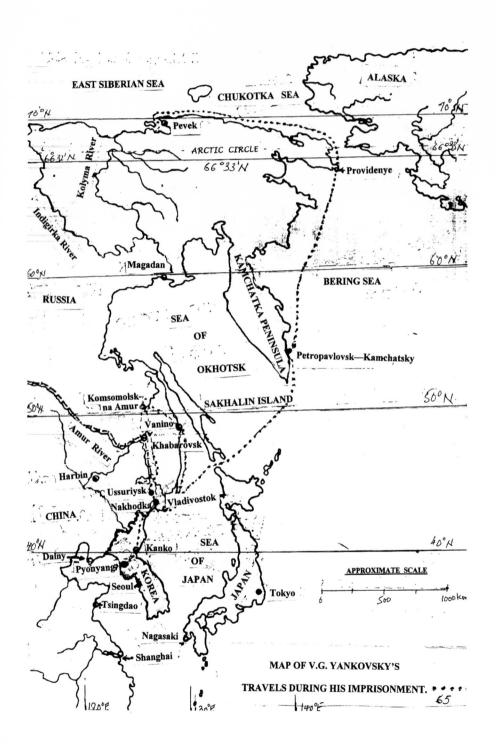

EAST SIBERIAN SEA ALASKA
CHUKOTKA SEA

70°N 70°N
Pevek

ARCTIC CIRCLE
66°31'N 66°33'N 66°33'N

Kolyma River

Indigirka River Providenye

60°N

Magadan BERING SEA

RUSSIA

SEA

OF

OKHOTSK KAMCHATKA PENINSULA

Petropavlovsk—Kamchatsky

Komsomolsk-na Amur SAKHALIN ISLAND 50°N

50°N

Vanino

Amur River Khabarovsk

Harbin

Ussuriysk

Nakhodka Vladivostok

CHINA

40°N SEA 40°N

Dalny Kanko OF

Pyongyang JAPAN JAPAN

KOREA Tokyo

Seoul APPROXIMATE SCALE

Tsingdao 0 500 1000 km

Nagasaki

Shanghai MAP OF V.G. YANKOVSKY'S

TRAVELS DURING HIS IMPRISONMENT. • • • •

120°E 130°E 140°E 65

Contents

Chapter 1 Transportation

They transported us like wild animals caged behind bars of a railway car. Dozens of our pale faces could be barely seen in the light of a single light bulb, whose glow was reflected in our eyes. Finger thick iron bars divided our freight car into two compartments.

Our carriage was making rhythmic sounds, as it rolled over the junctions between rails, passing snow-covered fields and dark tunnels cut through the steep hills of Korea on its way from Pyongyang to Vladivostok.

There were no windows in our car. A make-shift stove made from an oil barrel stood in its centre. Next to it two soldiers armed with automatic weapons sat on upturned boxes. Behind the bars stood a chamber pot latrine. The "passengers", all of them veterans of the recent war against Japan, sat behind the bars like chickens on a perch. Some of them were marauders, deserters, thieves and burglars, and some others were "political" prisoners, convicted under Article 58 of the Penal Code of the Russian Federation. Some were guilty of admiring foreign technology, others had cursed Stalin, others still had slept with captured

Japanese women, which was classified as "Betrayal of the Motherland", point 16 of the Article, punishable by 10 years imprisonment.

I had also been imprisoned for 10 years, despite the fact that I neither slept with a Japanese lass nor cursed Stalin. In fact, I trusted him at the time. My conviction was based on the fact that my father was the owner of a large estate near Vladivostok. He had horses, deer, plantations of the medicinal plant ginseng and fisheries. Fearing persecution following the Communist victory, he fled that area with his family (myself included) in 1922 and went to North-Eastern Korea where we lived right up to the beginning of the Second World War, which started in 1941. Naturally enough, we obeyed Japanese laws, which existed there at that time, but within a few days of Russia commencing hostilities against Japan in August 1945 I found my way to the headquarters of the 25th Russian Army in Manchuria and, having told the story of my life to its commanding officers, was accepted as an interpreter of Japanese and Korean languages.

The Chief of the Military council of the 25th Army Lt-General Lebedev solemnly assured me that all émigrés who had not committed crimes against the Soviet Union had been forgiven, and that dispensation applied not only to the young people but also to their parents. Lebedev gave me a job in the Special Division of his Army. I accompanied it to Pyongyang in September of 1945 and continued working till January 1946, when I was granted leave to visit my family in our holiday resort of Novina located in Korea's North-East.

CHAPTER 1

Novina had been created over a period of twenty years through the boundless energy of my parents and the help of us, their children, and next of kin. It started off as an empty plateau on the banks of a crystal-clear river flowing through a valley situated between steep Korean hills. We transformed it into a spectacular location.

We created alleys of poplars and white acacias, built striking "dachas" (holiday homes), a theatre, which also served as a clubhouse, a guests' dining room, tennis courts and an exotic hanging bridge over the fast flowing river Ompo. But that was not all. We also had an orchard, an apiary, a small dairy farm and an enclosure containing wild deer caught in the forest, whose soft horns called "pantui", used in Tibetan medicine, gave us sufficient income to cover most of our running expenses. Hunting was another profitable venture.

Novina was very popular as a holiday resort. Holiday-makers and tourists flocked to it from spring till late autumn of all pre-war years. They consisted of Asians and Europeans from large Manchurian, Chinese and Korean cities of Harbin, Tientsin, Shanghai and Seoul. Novina was widely known through the hot water springs of the nearby resort of Ompo and because of Lukomorye, a glorious ocean beach located 18 km away, where our family also had holiday facilities. We were incredibly popular even in Europe, and letters from that continent, addressed simply "Korea, Yankovsky" invariably reached their mark.

I had no letters from home during my war service in the 25th Army, but heard that all was well there. My wife was living with her parents in Novina expecting our baby. My youngest brother Yuri was working with me in Pyongyang and my younger brother Arseny worked for the Soviet Naval Intelligence in Seisin.(Chongjin in Korean)

When I applied for leave, my boss Colonel Demidov not only granted it but also decided to reward me for my services. He took me to a store containing captured enemy weapons and, knowing that I was a fervent hunter, let me pick hunting rifles of my choosing. I selected a Mauser rifle and a Browning automatic shotgun. Demidov told me that prior to going home I had to accompany a Captain Nikolayev on a trip to the town of Kanko where I was required to be his interpreter for three days. I vividly remember the first day of my trip home. It was the 24th of January 1946. The weather was absolutely brilliant following a recent snowfall. It was the birthday of my brother Yuri who was farewelling me at the Pyongyang railway station, but I noticed that he was uncharacteristically sad.

Having arrived in Kanko, we were having dinner in the officer's quarters, which comprised a large room with several neatly made up soldiers' beds and hunting rifles on the walls. My mate Nikolayev, a rosy-cheeked fellow with bulging grey eyes, put a magnum of Japanese sake on the table and was animatedly discussing a hunt on pheasants and wild goats. His idea was to organise a hunting expedition following the completion of our assignment, but I told him that I missed my wife and family and wanted to get going as soon as possible.

CHAPTER 1

Our discussion was interrupted by the diminutive figure of a Major who appeared at the entrance to our quarters and beckoned to Captain Nikolayev:

"Come and see me"—said he.

The captain left and I sat alone, reading our Army newssheet and anticipating a glass of sake and the dinner, which was being picked up by the commandant of our quarters. Nikolayev returned but, strangely, did not sit down and started to walk around the table instead... One circle, two, three...

"What's up?" said I, lifting my head from the paper.

He finally sat down, rested his head on his hand and said in an even, but I thought also sympathetic voice:

"Yee—s...You are in a hurry to get home, but I must arrest you instead . Empty your pockets."

"You must be joking!" exclaimed I incredulously. I really could not believe that he was serious.

But believe him I very soon did. With our commandant acting as a witness, Nikolayev confiscated all my documents, money and valuables and compiled an official deed, keeping the original and giving me a copy, which I later used instead of cigarette paper.. He warned me in a friendly manner that there had been an epidemic in the jail where I was being sent, but that the place had been thoroughly disinfected and therefore I had nothing to fear. "Take with you all the useful personal belongings"—said he. "It is likely that you would be detained for a month or two and will be released once the enquiries are concluded."

CHAPTER 1

I don't know whether my arrest had been planned or whether it was initiated at the moment of the appearance of the tiny major, but I have to concede that the whole operation was executed with great skill. Such tricks were always well rehearsed by the authorities.

Some time later, I recalled a odd episode, which took place a long time before I left Pyongyang. Brother Yuri and I who were renting a flat together with two Secret Service ("SMERSH" in Russian) officers, had a visit from a lieutenant who worked in the same department. The fellow was dead drunk and was barely coherent, but I had no difficulty in understanding what he was telling us. "Keep in mind, that you are being secretly watched...You may be arrested...It might be better to cross the 38th parallel (*the border between North and South Korea MH)*...Give it some thought..."

I was incensed. "Why on earth would I want to do that? I have led a blameless life and I honestly told my life story on the first day of my employment!" It occurred to me at the time that the lieutenant's performance was a ruse designed to get me into trouble, whereas the poor fellow was taking an incredible risk, as his warning would have most certainly landed him in jail. Not only did I not believe him, but I was also aware of the fact that a flight would jeopardise the welfare of my nearest and dearest who appeared to be safe at the time. It took me 17 years to find out from Yuri when I met him after our imprisonment that he was arrested the day after I left Pyongyang and was most probably still on my way to Kanko!..

CHAPTER 1

I was put into an old Japanese jail mentioned by Nikolayev, where I spent 11 months and not unexpectedly contacted spotted fever within a very few days of imprisonment. I was delirious and saw clear visions of my wife Irma and our local priest Father John Maximovich entering my cell. They spent a few minutes with me and told me before leaving that I ought to light a candle and say a prayer, after which the doors of my prison would fly open. I came to, but was unable to light the candle and turned to my window in which I saw Stalin standing just above the window-sill against the background of the starry sky and silently looking at me. I said:

"Why am I here, Joseph? What am I guilty of?"

He replied in an even muffled voice:

"You are not guilty. We have established your innocence and have given you the rank of a major general. You will get your uniform and shoulder straps at a meeting which is taking place at 11 o'clock tonight", said he, whereupon the Leader of all Nations suddenly disappeared from sight.

The top of my cell door consisted of a glass-enclosed grill and I had a good view of the corridor with a sentry armed with an automatic sub-machine gun marching up and down its length. He stopped in response to my knock.

"Yes. What do you want?"

"Don't you know that Stalin is organising a meeting?"

Not receiving a positive response I, despite my generally obedient disposition, grabbed a small timber tub and smashed the glass in my cell door scattering shards of glass all over the floor and sending the horrified soldier into flight. He was followed by the officer in charge of the guards who used to often chat with me, but must have decided that I went mad.

"I know, I know", said he, without saying anything about the glass, "but the meeting has been postponed till tomorrow. Have some sleep now."

I lay down and came to only two weeks later when an imprisoned Korean doctor with a deep scar (most likely the result of an interrogation) on his face was giving me an injection of half a litre of a nourishing liquid.

"You have a remarkably strong heart", said he. "Your temperature has been over 41 (Centigrade, over 106 Fahrenheit!) for a fortnight. I had no idea that you would pull through"...

It took me a long time to walk again after that illness...

Strange as it may seem, I was not officially under arrest, but merely "detained", which meant that having left the prison hospital I was only expected to sleep in my cell and was allowed to walk around the prison yard and do some reading. The head of the Investigation Unit major Novikov used to supply me with the works of Lenin and Marx's 'Das Kapital", which I had naturally never seen before. He spent a lot of time discussing politics with me and offered to write to my home telling my family that I was on a business trip and would very likely be soon home. He asked me to give Russian lessons to the Korean staff of the prison and fed me as if food was going out of style. He gave me army rations, the prison fare and some other food. My appetite after the illness was unbelievable, and I weighed more than ever before in my life. The balmy summer weather continued and nothing seemed to point towards a storm. The chief of the guards, a sergeant whom I knew quite well, told me several times that in confidence that he overheard his superiors say that I would be soon released.

However, an order for my arrest was issued in October 1946, followed by a court case. I was certain that I would be acquitted and was astonished to hear the verdict of six years imprisonment in the GULAG based on Article 58-4 of the penal code: "Assisting the activities of the International Bourgeoisie." I could barely stay on my feet. Why? Yes, I lived in Korea, which was a Japanese colony at the time. Yes, I paid taxes, which were used to finance the war against China and worked for the Postal Service, where my duties involved listening to Russian radio broadcasts. That activity was classified as "eavesdropping" and "gathering of economic information"—a conduct akin to espionage, although an open radio broadcast does not contain any secrets and is meant for the whole world.

On return to my cell I collapsed for the first time in my life and barely managed to crawl to a mug containing some water. However, I recovered and wrote a statement requesting a retrial.

I was taken to Pyongyang in January 1947. On that trip I was handcuffed and was chained to five other prisoners, all of whom were Koreans. Following that I was taken to Seisin (*currently known as*

Chongjin MH) where I had to confront my father, who, as I had found out, was also in prison.

A second trial took place following my return from Pyongyang, which dealt with the revision of the original proceedings. I was still hopeful of an acquittal, as I had thoroughly explained my innocence in my application, until my former colleague lieutenant–colonel Boozareff approached me during the recess and whispered:

"Be ready for the result. The district authorities have reviewed you case and found that six years was not enough. They are demanding ten. We are helpless... A great pity..."

My legs felt as if they were filled with lead. A customary "tenner"!

And here I was—travelling heaven knows where, why and what for?

I am certain that the imprisonment of the White Russian emigrant youth was a terrible mistake, a tragic paradox. Considering my case, I could never accept our defeat in the ill-fated Russo-Japanese War of 1904-1905, a defeat over which many Japanese gloated quite offensively. I read all I could about that debacle, written both by Russian and foreign authors. I often fantasised that I was attacking and mercilessly slaughtering their cavalry in the fields of Manchuria or commanding a destroyer, which was torpedoing a Japanese battleship...

Many of our number wrote to the Soviet Consulate asking to be sent as volunteers to fight the Germans, and all who could selflessly and unselfishly offered their services to the Red Army from the moment it attacked Japan. We had an old dream of offering a substantial help to our Motherland because of our knowledge of languages, customs and local conditions. Moreover, we could help to develop the friendship between our compatriots and the indigenous people of Korea and Manchuria. But despite all this, the vast majority of us were subjected to trials by military tribunals, based on the fact that we lived on foreign soil. Practically all of us were mowed down by those kangaroo courts, which in addition bestowed upon us the stigma of the "enemy of the people". During all the terrifying years of imprisonment, transportation and Gulag camps I always had one word indelibly imprinted on my mind: **WHY?**

...Our carriage was rocking and rolling. Some sentries put aside their automatic weapons and broke up coal with a blunt axe, others smoked or dozed. Some of us were allowed to join them late at night at the stove for a smoke and yarn, when a visit from the commanding officers was unlikely. Some of them were clearly decent fellows who felt sorry for us. Little did they know what risks they were running, as at that same time my former workmate from Pyongyang, short and pock-marked lieutenant Vladimir Rozanov, was urgently whispering into my ear:

"Let's ask them to let us join them at the stove to get some warmth. We will then knock them out and kill them with their axe, grab their weapons, break down the floor or the wall and do a runner. Nobody will know till it is light, and we'll be gone..."

It was a viable proposition, but that meant taking advantage of those lads' humanity and killing them with a dirty woodchopper. Doesn't he understand what he is proposing? But Vladimir is looking at me from his corner with a wild burning gaze and I can know that he will never understand my feelings of compassion for the sentries or my notion of decency. I had to answer with a weighty argument.

"No, now is not the time" -whisper I—"There is snow everywhere now. They will track us like rabbits, and that will be it. Let's wait till we get to our destination and then think about an escape. I am sure that we'll have many more better chances than this one."

My former boss colonel Demidov paid us a visit before our prison train left Pyongyang. He wore a tidy knee-length sheepskin coat and well polished boots. Having examined our carriage he gave us a condescending friendly smile and said:

"All is well, fellows! You'll have a comfortable trip!"

He pretended not to have seen me, which gave him an excuse to ignore my presence, despite the fact that I worked for him for almost six months and recently carried out a rather delicate operation on his behalf.

Demidov was pleasant and ingratiating when one day he invited me into his office and asked me to sit down.

"I want to ask you to do me a favour"—said he. "You know that there are some Japanese families from Manchuria and Korea in the building of the local school who are waiting to be sent home. We are, feeding them, of course, but the Koreans steal some of their rations. I heard that they are short of rice, which is as important to them as bread is to us. I also heard that they still have quite a bit of jewellery hidden away and the Koreans and our soldiers, so to speak, help themselves to...To cut a long story short, I would like you as our senior interpreter to see them and have a bit of a chat. You could offer them a sort of an exchange, if you get my meaning. Let them get together some gold and, well, some rings perhaps, and we in return could organise some rice. Do you see what I mean?"

I went to the small school located in a building constructed of red brick, where hundreds of Japanese men, women and children dressed in their national dress (kimonos), suits and overcoats were lying cheek by jowl on the floor of the hallway. They were surrounded by their suitcases, travelling-bags and packs and looked pale, thin, downtrodden and humiliated, with despair clearly showing in their dark brown eyes. One could not deny that they lorded over the locals for a number of years. But was it their personal fault or the fault of their aggressive government and military? These people were merely sent to populate the conquered lands...

Nevertheless, they remained Japanese, even in this dramatic abnormal situation and showed their customary order and discipline, having elected group leaders whose orders they followed without questioning. The leaders spoke with me with courtesy and respect due to the representative of the authorities. Yes, they said, accompanying their words with respectful bows, things are rather difficult. The Koreans are vindictive. They conduct searches and confiscate even personal belongings. However, they still have some valuables, which they would like to exchange. Yes, rice would be very good. Come in the evening, sensei *(teacher)* and we shall give you all our valuables...

That evening I delivered to them ten bags of rice on a truck driven by a group of soldiers, whereupon the senior Japanese handed me a heavy parcel wrapped in a piece of cloth. I went to Demidov's office where I met with four cordially smiling colonels, each of them a head of a subsection, seated around a square table. Having been asked to join them, I put the parcel on the table and unwrapped its contents. The room was well lit, and we could see the glitter of gold chains, pocket and wrist watches, pendants and a lot of rings with precious stones: rubies, sapphires, amethysts and turquoise. I thought that these valuables were about to be listed and entered into a ledger, but instead of that I saw eight hands grasping at the valuables. The colonels were feverishly digging through the pile and grabbing individual pieces.

"Listen, I am going on leave to Ussurijsk"—said one—"these are for my Mary!"

"Hey! Go easy"—was the reply—"I am also going on leave!"

"No, that won't do!" -piped in the third—"Let's evenly divide up the whole lot!"

It took less than ten minutes for the large pile to turn into four small ones—one in front of each of the bosses, except for two small items not made out of gold and not containing any coloured jewellery. They were a platinum ring with a large diamond and a ladies' watch whose face was surrounded with small diamonds. I gave the by now hot and sweaty chiefs an incredulous look:

"Who is taking these, comrades? This is platinum with diamonds!"

However, neither the remaining jewellery nor my words made any impression.

"What do we want this glass for? The metal is dull and the stones are colourless. Take them if you like."

I hesitated. Should I take them or refuse the offer? What will I prove by my honesty?

I looked at my boss after a short pause, and he nodded approvingly. I picked up the two items with a feigned air of indifference, knowing full well that they were worth about half of the rest of the jewellery, and nonchalantly put them in my pocket, after which I excused myself and left the gathering. I was sure at the time that I was about to go on leave and would be able to make a decent present to my wife Irma.

However, my personal belongings were confiscated after the first trial under somewhat unusual circumstances. Being an interpreter, I got to know the trial procedure quite well and was aware that although it was not possible to alter the verdict after the trial, the prisoner was allowed the last word, a last plea. Therefore in my last plea I asked for my personal belongings to be sent to my wife who was about to have a child and would be destitute without my help. The members of the tribunals realised that they forgot to order the confiscation of my personal property! "Add to the verdict: *with confiscation of all personal property!*" -instructed they the secretary of the tribunal....

Our train was taking us ever further away from our previous lives, but memories of the past and its episodes stayed with us. We were all live flesh and blood, with our individual fates and accompanying dramas. Most people told their life stories, the reasons for their imprisonment, including the article of the penal code used to convict them and the duration of the sentence. The majority had to serve ten or more years, but we also had a "lucky" fellow in our midst who was sentenced to "only" three years and was the envy of the rest of us. He was a skinny yellow-faced Korean, an inhabitant of Pyongyang and though most certainly not a Soviet citizen, carried a conviction for a political crime. The most despicable paragraph of the dreaded Article 58 was, in my opinion, number 12, which dealt with somebody who knew of a transgression but failed to report it. That paragraph was responsible for the appearance of a cohort of relatives, friends and acquaintances turned traitors, even though it envisaged a "childish" maximum penalty of, I seem to recall, five years. It seems that the Pyongyang flat of our "lucky devil" had been visited by some murky characters wanted by the authorities, although he insisted that he knew nothing about it. However, the security people established that he knew who his visitors were, but failed to denounce them. He was arrested, convicted and was being transported despite the fact that he was ill and having told us his story spent most of the time lying silently in the corner. Others envied him, but he did not even survive as far as the Russian border. In the morning of the fourth day of our journey he was called to get his breakfast, but was already dead, and was taken off the train when we were changing trains in Kraskino.

The man who refused to become a traitor lost his life as a result of that fact, and he was one of many. A question of principle arises here: on what grounds did the security services known as NKVD-MGB run by Stalin and Beria arrest people who were not their citizens and sentence them to slave labour in Gulag camps in the Kolyma, Siberia and other places? The reason was that they had the power to do it and Stalin, Beria and their accomplices ordered these actions without the slighted regard for their legality. I am not talking of prisoners of war here, as they have been customarily retained by the winning side since time immemorial, but about civilians who had not taken part in hostilities.

And what about those who were automatically sent into slavery as a result of a mistake? Let me quote a couple of examples of such dastardly lawlessness.

In my capacity as an interpreter I took part in the investigation of a case of a group of Japanese who had been leading lights in the Kanto Province, who were transported from there to be tried in Pyongyang when our 25th Army moved from Manchuria to Korea.

That group consisted of 13 men. Four of them were senior Area officers, four others occupied senior District positions and a further five had been village cops. None of them committed any direct crimes against the USSR, although their position could have (theoretically) enabled them to organise armed resistance to the Red Army. That was, to be honest, a very long shot.

I was working with the Senior Investigator by the name of Vladimir Butsky, who was relieved when all these "cases" were coming to the end. His task was to write a charge sheet covering each of these men and to send them to the Section Head captain Ignashenko for his consideration. Butsky had already completed 12 such sheets, but had doubts about the thirteenth folder which contained material about a policeman by the name of Kawahara, who spent his short service in that position as an officer in charge of a small area overseen by the so-called "Forest Police", which had no political role whatsoever. I could see that Volodya *(short for "Vladimir" MH)* was having severe doubts.

"You know, I think that Kawahara is not involved in this business at all. We ought to separate him from the rest and send him to the displaced persons' camp for repatriation to Japan, which is about to start."

With these words he put the thirteenth file aside.

The door of our office flew open just as he was doing so, and captain Ignashenko appeared on the threshold. He was pale, with dark circles under the eyes and his hair was in a mess. He sat down and clutched his head.

"Hell, I had too much to drink yesterday! My head is aching! Yes, we did hit the bottle a bit too hard!"

We expressed our condolences, as befitted two underlings, whereupon Vladimir pointed to the files.

CHAPTER 1

"Here you are, comrade captain. I finished my indictment of the twelve, but I think that the thirteenth, Kawahara, is completely innocent and ought to be excluded from the proceedings. Have a look for yourself."

Ignashenko cast an indifferent and one might even say disgusted glance at the papers whilst sitting opposite Vladimir and still clutching his temples. His condition did not allow him to concentrate. Finally he ruffled his hair and said:

"No compromising material, did you say? To hell with this guy! Think of something. The tribunal will decide whether he is innocent or guilty...."

Senior lieutenant Butsky obediently nodded his head and started to "think", even though being a decent well-educated native of Kiev, he found it difficult to obey the order. Butsky was different from many others. For example, his colleague lieutenant Podgorny who was drunk during one of the interrogation sessions, tried to extinguish a cigarette butt on the forehead of a terrified middle-aged Japanese who was frozen with horror at that treatment. I am sure I was taking a grave risk when I shouted:

"How dare you! What a shame! Do you forget that you are a Red Army officer?!"

"How dare you shout at me?" –shouted back an equally incensed Podgorny.

We became enemies after that day. I think that he could have engineered my arrest...

CHAPTER 1

The group of thirteen finally went on trial before a "troika" (*a tribunal consisting of three members MH*) in December of 1945, which conducted its sittings in a large hall, behind a table covered with red woollen cloth. The tribunal secretary occupied a smaller table next to the troika and the interpreters (I and a Japanese half-caste by the name of Toizumi), sat on the other side of the troika at a table covered with a green tablecloth.

The accused sat on benches, with the front one occupied by the Area officers who were the main accused, followed by the District chiefs, with five lesser lights, skinny and yellow like a dried cuttlefish Kawahara included, languishing on the third. They all sat motionless looking at the tribunal with a look reminiscent of a hypnotised frog gazing at a snake. I was full of expectations that the court was going to establish the facts, free the innocent thirteenth accused and send him to the displaced persons' camp.

Regrettably, however, nothing of the kind took place and, in fact, there was practically no court examination as such. The chairman of the tribunal acquainted its members with the preliminary investigation and made a solemn announcement of the standard sentences: the front bench got 20 years, the second—15 and the last—10. This, of course, included Kawahara...

It is quite possible that but for captain Ignashenko's hangover, Kawahara could have avoided the Siberian Gulag, a place from which many never retuned...

That was the first example. The second one concerns a native of Harbin, one Ivan Silinsky who worked on an experimental Soviet-style state farm on the outskirts of the town with a Russian defector by the name of Galitsky. There were a lot of people like him in Manchuria. Galitsky was being sought by SMERSH (*a branch of the Secret Police, MH*) after the Reds occupied Harbin, but he managed to give them the slip. A SMERSH captain called Yermolayev befriended Silinsky and, having found out that Ivan knew Galitsky asked him to help his Motherland to catch the filthy traitor and to report the results of his efforts to him. Yermolayev asked Silinsky to come on a particular evening to the Harbin Sailing Club, located on the banks of the River Sungari, and to wait for him on a park bench. "I'll most certainly get there"—he promised.

Silinsky took his assignment very seriously indeed, as he was eager to help his compatriots and through them his Motherland. He was one of many émigrés who risked their lives for that cause. Not having found Galitsky, he nevertheless kept his word (he was, by the way the son of a priest) and came to the arranged meeting at the Sailing Club. Silinsky was particularly looking forward to the meeting, as he developed a deep respect for his new acquaintance. He was early and started his patient wait on a park bench near the pier. Various motor boats kept leaving the pier, some of them heading for the opposite bank of the river and others—for the warships stationed in the river. He also noticed a sentry who was pacing up and down along the river bank

The sentry got suspicious of the stranger's presence. "Why have you been sitting here all this time?" he asked.

"I am waiting for captain Yermolayev. I have to report something to him."

"You must be nuts!" – said the soldier, touching his forehead– "Get the hell out of here before you get into real trouble!"

Ivan ignored the warning and kept smoking and waiting for his "mate".

A car arrived a short while later and disgorged an unknown SMERSH officer who gave Ivan a suspicious glance.

"What are you waiting for here?" – asked he.

"I am waiting for captain Yermolayev. I have a report to make."

"OK, come with me to the warship to make your report."

The officers on the ship asked Ivan to write his life story *(a standard practice of SMERSH. MH)*. "Make sure that you don't omit anything"– was the command.

Silinsky made sure that he did not miss a thing, one of the items of interest for his new friends being that he had worked in the Russian Volunteer Corps in Shanghai, guarding the British Concession in that city.

Having read and studied Ivan's story, they sentenced him to 15 years imprisonment in the Kolyma *(North of the Arctic Circle in Siberia MH)* Gulag, where he was expected to participate in the development of that region, starting with his arrival in late autumn in the freezing Far Eastern city of Khabarovsk wearing a felt hat and sand shoes!

CHAPTER 1

It seems that the sentry on the banks of the Sungari who was telling him to go was a nice bloke...

This was one of many such callous "misunderstandings". Here is one more: SMERSH was looking for a fascist called Migunov, but got hold of another person who had a similar name of **Melgunov.** A wrong man! Do you think they took him off the warship and returned him to his family? Fat chance! He also received a "tenner", to be served in Magadan (*Russia's Far East MH*). The irony of it was that the fascist Migunov was set free after many years, but the innocent Melgunov literally lost his head when a helicopter lopped it off during his stay as a slave labourer in the tundra.

Human life meant nothing to the fiends who put themselves in charge of it...

We finally arrived at our destination and having disembarked one windy cold February night at a goods' station near Vladivostok called "The First River" (*"Pervaya Rechka" in Russian MH*), took a long march along the steep, cobble stone covered streets of that town, accompanied by armed guards. In that hungry post-war year of 1947, my native town, which I had not seen for 25 years, struck me as impoverished, pitiful and completely strange. People were appallingly dressed and looked utterly destitute. Women wore huge head-scarves and coarse military boots, with most lugging heavy bags slung over their shoulders. Everybody was in a hurry. A truck driver was standing next to his frozen vehicle and vainly attempted to start it by cranking the starter handle whilst uttering foul obscenities...

Our detachment marched past them in a disorganised manner, surrounded by armed guards and savage dogs, but I noticed that nobody took the slightest bit of notice of our plight, which made me think that these scenes were commonplace here and the inhabitants of Vladivostok were quite used to them.

We finally found ourselves entering the arched brick gates of an old prison, which greeted us with its dark exterior, its mouldy smell and a stench of carbolic acid. The atmosphere was that of an inescapable gloom. Our rations consisted of a small piece of damp black bread full of bran and a bowl of thin broth, garnished with pea-sized pieces of uncleaned potatoes.

A week later I found myself in my first transit camp, the notorious "Sixth Kilometre," located on the First River. We stayed in long low barracks on the side of a hill, surrounded by barbed wire, with watchtowers on the corners of its perimeter, looking for all the world like little peasant huts on stilts. An obligatory "Special Purpose Building" (*the Russian acronym for it is "BUR"- MH)*- completed the "architectural ensemble". The prisoners were woken up at 6am with a blood-curdling sound of a rail suspended on a piece of rope being struck by a guard, followed by a line-up and a formation of work-groups consisting of five men each. Finally, the issue of a miner's hack, shovel and wheelbarrow was made to each inmate.

That regime did not last long for me, as about a hundred of us were organised into groups of five and sent to a proper working camp in the Diomid Bay, on the southern outskirts of Vladivostok. We passed

Pushkinskaya Street on our way, on one of whose corners stood house number 49, which used to belong to my "Nana *("Baba" in Russian–MH)* Alya", my maternal grandmother, the wife of a merchant, Alexandra Dimitriyevna Sheveleva. I was born in that house and all our family, including children and parents, used to visit it on our motor cruiser. We would leave our country property in Sedemi, which was situated on the Yankovsky Peninsula. The reasons for our visits were many and varied. We would go to the races, go to the circus and attend High School, as well as simply come to see Baba Alya and do some shopping. My father's Vladivostok office was also located in that house. Now it looked aged, sick and neglected, like an old abandoned friend. I found out later that it had been turned into a communal abode for eleven families.

Diomid Bay was filled with the cries of seagulls and smelt of the sea and fish. Small vessels were moored at the pier. Steam locomotives were noisily carrying out their manoeuvres on a railway station, which was being supplied by a small dusty prison camp sitting on the side of a hill. We used to march to that camp under the supervision of two soldiers armed with rifles with attached bayonets. The streets were practically empty and the badly dressed pedestrians carrying something, which looked like provisions in their bags looked harassed and were always in a hurry. But good God! Did we envy them! They were FREE and were able to go where they pleased, but what about us? And we were no thieves or bandits, but mostly former POWs of the Germans or émigrés like me.

CHAPTER 1

Despite the vigilance of our guards we managed to pick up cigarette butts using sticks or nails as simple tools; we would put them into small containers, extract the tobacco and roll our own cigs out of old newsprint, to the accompaniment of plaintive shouted pleas from our mates to let them have a half or a quarter of the treasure...

Our work consisted of loading bulk cement or lime into fifty-tonne carriages, which left a residue of these materials in our noses, ears, on the necks and in all creases and crevices of our clothing. All that, and not a chance to have a bath or to change the filthy clothing. The only way to reduce the quantity of dirt was to bash our coats and pants against the power pole located in the yard of our camp, to the accompaniment of the ever-present thought: "Why, oh why?!", followed by: "Well, this is still better than jail. I always have the chance of a last resort to take a run-up towards the smooth power pole polished by our clothing and to crack my skull against it!"

I felt that I could not last long, because the food rations were similar to the ones in jail, but the work was heavy and exhausting. For instance, we had to unload railway carriages full of boxes of car batteries, each weighing between 90 and 127 kilograms. The four of us had to place each of them on our backs and unload about 100 of these beasts per shift, to the accompaniment of the cheerful calls from our foreman: "Into it, men! Show what you are worth! Don't forget that you are being given a special gourmet treat to-night!"

CHAPTER 1

The "gourmet treat" consisted of a sliver of bluish-grey coloured barley porridge, which was slippery like soap and contained very few calories. The whole thing was one big confidence trick...

These conditions resulted in all prisoners developing night blindness based on a vitamin deficiency, with prisoners stumbling around in the dusk and running into each other. The foreman managed to get some evil smelling fish oil to treat the best workers, and a medical orderly would give each of them a spoonful of this vile stuff at the end of the shift. However, in order to share the medication with their less fortunate mates, they would not swallow it but run into the hut and spit it out into a common bowl made of an old tin, so that everybody could dip a tiny piece of bread into that mess and make something resembling a toast out of the resulting soggy piece.

Once a week some prisoners including myself were sent to the jail to fetch provisions, and every time, alas in vain, I hoped to run into my cousin Tanya who, according to rumour, was serving her time in that establishment. Our mates provided us, messengers, with deep hidden pockets sewn onto the insides of our pants with strict instructions to fill them with any foodstuffs we could lay our hands on, such as salted goby and other small fish, but most frequently with soy oil-cake. I was amazed when during one of my "hunting episodes" during which I was filling up my pockets with my loot whilst sitting in the corner of a truck, I saw my guard surreptitiously shaking his open palm, hidden behind his back, in my direction. "Fill it up", was the unmistakable secret message. I realised then that the guards were also hungry....

We started thinking of escape, as it was obvious that we could not survive under the existing conditions. A group of prospective fugitives appears to have materialised out of thin air. It included myself, a Volodya Rozanoff, who had been convicted for trying to escape abroad, a son of a general by the name of Igor Litvinov, and three of my compatriots from Manchuria: a former student of the Harbin Lyceum by the name of Kolya Kuchma, a middle-aged hunter from Pogranichnaya railway station, called Grisha Ryabovich and Fedya Shepkin, a young agile and bright member of a family of hunters.

Our preparation for an escape lasted for a fairly long time and we were waiting for a suitable moment to make the run. However, some low life got wind of our plans and betrayed our group.

Our working group was disbanded. Shepkin and Ryabovich were returned to jail, I and Rozanoff were sent back to Pervaya Rechka and young Kuchma and Litvinov stayed put at Diomid Bay. A middle-aged quiet guard walked me and Rozanoff across the city to the "Sixth's Kilometre" guard house, which was already familiar to us. The receiving officers took one look at our accompanying papers, exchanged a few whispered words and immediately sent me alone to the "Special Zone" *(the Russian acronym for it is ZUR. MH)*, situated at the far end of the prison camp, which was surrounded by barbed wire.

I was looking through the barbed wire at the dark huts hoping to see a familiar face. I knew that my friend Eugene August Ellers was imprisoned here, but had no idea that I was about to meet my father. It seems that the International Brotherhood of **Zeks** *(Russian acronym for* *the prisoners of the GULAG, MH)* had already broadcast the message: "Somebody has been returned from Diomid Bay and locked up in the ZUR." It is even possible that my name was also broadcast, since I could see Dad resolutely marching towards the barbed wire. He looked quite OK, despite the fact that he had already been imprisoned for more than six months. He was dressed in his customary "uniform" of a service jacket and khaki coloured breeches, sporting his traditional moustache and even wearing his usual hat with some kind of a feather. Dad stopped at the wire reminiscent of the one, which was surrounding our deer enclosure in our estate in Novina, and thrust his hand through its circular opening.

"How do you like all this"—were his first words—"Remember how you used to argue with me?"

He was absolutely right. Argue I did, and often quite vehemently, at that. It sometimes came to a point where one of us would leave the dinner table and walk out of the room. But in my defence I must emphatically say that the overwhelming majority of the émigré youth of those days ardently believed that things were good "at home in Russia" and that we had nothing to fear, not even those of us who, albeit unwillingly, served the Japanese. We all believed that that work would equip us with useful knowledge in our future service for our Motherland. Moreover, that conviction was being reinforced by the clandestine radio station called "Otchisna" (*Russian for "Motherland" MH*). Young people used to listen to its broadcasts, despite the risk of being thrown into the torture chambers of the Japanese Secret Service, known as "The Gendarmerie", and to share their contents in whispered tones with their friends. However, their elders urged them not to believe that propaganda: "We shall all be in deep trouble should, God forbid, the Reds ever occupy Manchuria or Korea", said they.

The other prisoners started listening to my conversation with Dad, and we switched to English. I asked:

"What are those mountain tops west of us, Dad?"– asked I. "Is it the Blue Ridge, with Manchuria behind it? Do you think that I shall be on the other side of the border if I reach it?".

The old man made a barely perceptive movement of his head in that direction and stroked his moustache in a characteristic manner well known to me since childhood:

"You are absolutely right, Son, but do be careful, as the risk involved is enormous. It would have been different had the two of us been in it together. Do think it over..." He then continued in Russian:

"Ellers and I will ask the authorities to let you meet us in our hut tonight. I received a parcel and we should be able to have a nice cup of coffee. Do you still smoke, by the way?"

I knew that my answer would upset him but replied: "Yes, Dad", because I was dying for a smoke. Father went back to his hut and came out carrying a piece of bread and an old sock, which had been darned many times, filled with "makhorka", an inferior type of tobacco, and handed over his present through an opening in the wire fence. His last words were:

"I hear that your group is being transported somewhere tomorrow. Take heart. Don't forget that a young son is expecting you at home.

You are still young and they will let you go one day. As for me, my chances are not as good..."

An overseer saw the scene of our farewell and was approaching us rapidly panting and shouting like a maniac:

"Stop that conversation! Leave the wire fence! Get away from each other!"

Dad waved to me and went towards his hut.

I was given my normal rations that night but had to stay on my own in the "ZUR", and about forty of us were woken up by a shouted command: "Collect your belongings and get ready for transport!" We were assembled into a marching formation and stood at the gates to the labour camp, where I caught my last ever glimpse of my father. He was heading for our group only to be stopped in his tracks by a rude shout from a guard: "Where the hell are you going!? Don't you dare go near them!" He walked back and stood at the side of the road while we were being loaded into a truck in groups of five, and he and I exchanged glances. I wish I knew what was going on at that moment in the heart of that Iron Man...

Volodya Ryazanov and I sat next to each other and he pointed out to me a long brick hut, which housed the Officers' School where he studied before the war with Japan. That former lieutenant of the Red Army was now being transported with the rest of us prisoners in a rocky truck as punishment for the pleasure of having lived for a couple of months with a Japanese mistress...

Chapter 2: Forbidden Zone—The Zone Of Death

It was the second half of May 1947, the time of year when the sun was getting warmer and the trees growing on both sides of the Vladivostok—Ussurijsk Highway were beginning to flower. The prison trucks carrying me and other inmates of the Gulag left Nadezhdinskaya railway station, turned left and arrived an hour later at Tavricahanka, a settlement in one of the corners of Amur Bay located opposite the mouth of the Suifoon River. Having heard its name, I remembered an old story about how my father, accompanied by members of his private militia, unmasked and caught a band of Hung Hu Tse (*Chinese "Red Beard" bandits, who were the scourge of Korea and Manchuria.–MH*). The bandits wore soot-covered rags, which convincingly disguised them as coal miners, but Father noticed their well-groomed hands and saw through the ruse. That old story went back to the days when Dad was the owner of the prosperous Yankovsky Peninsula and was in charge of the militia protecting the Posyet Region.

CHAPTER 2

However, Yankovsky Peninsula owes its name to my Polish grandfather Michael, son of Yan *("Ivanovich" in Russian–MH)* Yankovsky, a descendant of the ancient clan of Novina, who was sentenced by the Russian Tsarist Government to penal servitude in the Transbaikal Region for his participation in the Polish Uprising of 1863. He was allowed to leave his prison as a result of the 1868 Amnesty and to live as a free man in that region, but had no right to return to his native Poland.

In 1874 he went to the Far East as a member of a scientific expedition led by his friend and former fellow political prisoner professor Benedikt Dubovsky. That move was followed by five years as manager of gold mines on the Askold Island.

He married a Russian woman by the name of Olga Lukinichna Kuznetsova in 1877 and in 1879 established a horse stud on the western shores of the Amur Bay, 30km from Vladivostok. There he produced a magnificent Far Eastern Horse as a result of many years of skilful interbreeding between Asian and European horses. Michael Yankovsky also tamed and bred some priceless spotted wild deer and established a plantation of normally wild-growing ginseng, the first such plantation in Russia. But that was not all.

Yankovsky discovered archaeological sites belonging to a prehistoric culture, which has been named after him. Finally, he gave his name to scores of butterflies, caterpillars and several subspecies of birds. Little wonder therefore, that the Peninsula where he conducted his activities also bears his name.

CHAPTER 2

My father Yuri (George) Michailovich Yankovsky inherited his father's estate, which existed for a total of forty one years. However, Yuri was forced to abandon that model enterprise due to the Bolshevik Revolution and had to emigrate to Korea, thus completing a strange circle of events: My grandfather was sentenced to penal servitude by the Tsar for his revolutionary activities, and eighty years later his son and grandchildren were sent to the Gulag by Stalin...

When I arrived to my ancestral lands in 1947, a prison camp surrounded by a timber fence and adorned by four watch towers stood on the outskirts of local coalmines, and the Tavrichanka settlement. It started off as a prison camp for Japanese POWs and had been transformed into a transit camp for incorrigible offenders awaiting transportation to the Far North. I and my colleagues found ourselves in that category.

An old uninhabited house stood in the centre of the camp, together with a few long low huts, a kitchen-cum dining room and a guardhouse, which also housed the prison administration. There was just one toilet for all the prisoners and it was located, halfway along the prison's eastern wall, near the so-called "forbidden zone."

The forbidden zone consisted of a three to four metre wide strip of land encircling the internal wall of the camp and separated from it by a metre fence adorned with barbed wire. Anybody attempting to cross it received a bullet from one of the guard towers. The administration made sure that the "zone" was kept in a pristine condition, which allowed the guards to see even the footprints of a cat. That was a "tabu" zone, a zone of death in the true sense of that word. However, the fence surrounding the camp was far from an ordinary structure. Five rows of barbed wire supported by curved steel posts were sitting on the top of it, which turned the rows of wire towards the camp. Anybody trying to climb the fence would find his head hitting several top curved rows, which made the fence practically impenetrable. Volodya and I had a good look at the situation and realised that things were very difficult indeed...

During our very first night in the camp we were attacked by a bunch of criminal thugs, who nearly strangled us while we were asleep and robbed us of our bread and tobacco rations. We retaliated the following morning by attacking them in the prison yard, which resulted in me receiving a knife wound just below an elbow. We complained to the commandant of our camp, a powerfully built Ukrainian, about the intolerable conduct of the criminal element and showed him my wound. However, his phlegmatic response was: "When a mob of sheep is made up of a few different mobs, fights start at first, but they soon get used to each other"...These thoughts of the great man strengthened our conviction that our only salvation lay in an escape.

That was easier said than done, of course. We decided to escape at night, provided we were not going to be sent to work during the day. The idea was to find a ladder, short circuit the lights and jump to freedom. We were very careful, since we would be done for had our attempt been discovered. The administration relied on the services of career criminals incarcerated with us to look after such matters. They walked around the camp day and night armed with heavy sticks and would at least maim us. These thugs received a privileged treatment, better food rations and willingly served as unofficial "police" to keep their perks.

I found some shelves in the kitchen of the old house and proceeded, with Volodya standing guard, to pull them apart with the aid of an old piece of iron and put together a crude ladder, whose length I estimated from the observation of the fence. My intention was to make it long enough to reach above the steel posts supporting the barbed wire on the fence. The job finished, I buried the ladder under some sawdust in the attic of the house.

In one of the huts we found some string, which was being used by a group of aged prisoners whose job it was to make fishing nets. Volodya pinched a roll of strong string, which he used to make a rope to which we were going to attach a piece of wire for sabotaging the wire of the electrified fence. Unfortunately, just as we were in the process of weaving our rope, two grubby heads belonging to army deserters appeared in the opening to the attic. Their owners were one Vaska Krivonos (*meaning "Broken Nose" in Russian MH*), who did actually have a broken nose, and Vovka, a sullen lad who before his enlistment had been a small-time crook and a thief. The pair immediately understood what we were up to and told us that they wanted to join us and would denounce us unless we complied. We thus had no choice but to accept that pair into our company.

CHAPTER 2

Vaska Krivonos suggested that we get in touch with professional criminals, as, according to him, they could be relied upon not to betray us and to join us in the escape or offer some useful advice. In the evening we paid a visit to the criminals' hut and held a palaver in its special "privileged" corner separated from the rest of the room by a bed sheet. Our interlocutor was a sullen character with a thick dark beard who was accompanied by two of his mates. He listened to our story and rasped:

"Too risky. It could work if you were to tunnel under a watchtower, but your plan means that you have a big chance of being shot. We take a risk when there is a ninety percent chance of success, but you have less than ten. Give it a go anyway. We know nothing".

And true to their word they did not turn us in...

It was getting close to the end of May. We twice attempted to escape, but were in each case let down by the wire, which was intended to short circuit the electrified fence. It would only cause a slight flicker of the lights and would melt in a flurry of sparks before causing a blackout. Each failure caused us to rush into the darkness like a bunch of frightened hares and to drop the ladder, which was, however, always hidden by somebody, thus avoiding a general alarm.

I was starting to make a third ladder out of the remaining shelves and was spotted by a skinny prisoner who called himself Ivan. He was a convicted marauder from the city of Diaren, who forced us to allow him to join our group, increasing it to five people.

CHAPTER 2

Needless to say, an escape from a prison camp is an extremely risky business. Hundreds of people milled around it by day, but no loitering was allowed after the sounding of the retreat. However, many inmates were suffering from gastric problems caused by hunger and malnutrition, and the single toilet meant for only fifteen people was always overcrowded. Therefore we always took refuge on its seats when the unofficial "policemen" bearing their heavy clubs made their unwelcome appearance.

The toilet abutted the "forbidden zone" and at night fall I used to dig out my ladder from underneath the wooden shavings and hide it against the wall of the latrine. We managed to find a replacement for the first two skinny bits of wire, in the form of a metre long piece of thin cable with two nuts attached to its ends, and tied it to the end of our jury-made rope.

Ten days of unsuccessful attempts at an escape have taught us that the pre-dawn hours offered the best chance for a dash to freedom. That was the time after the last patrol with guard dogs, a time when the fog was rising from the sea and the guards who keenly felt the cold in their watch towers would cover their openings with straw bags and, perhaps, even take a nap.

Our hour finally came after 3 am on the 31st of May 1947. The visits to the latrine had stpped and the "cops" had temporarily disappeared. **Time**...We are scared, our skin is crawling, but there is no going back.

Go!!!

CHAPTER 2

Volodka races out of the latrine and throws the rope with the attached cable across the barbed wire. The cable entwines around the steel wires, followed by a brilliant flash of light and darkness a few moments later. However, we had all that before: darkness followed by a few flickers and a return of light. Therefore we waited for one, two and, finally, three seconds, but it stayed dark. Those were the most frightening moments, as we were knowingly putting ourselves in harm's way... I grabbed the ladder built for the third escape attempt and took a step into the "Zone of Death." Should the lights have recovered, I would have been a perfect target for the sentries on all four towers. That thought was immediately overtaken by another, no less frightening than the first: will the ladder reach beyond the top of the steel support of the barbed wire? If it won't, we are all doomed, since there is no way we can climb over the overhanging fence.

Around my neck I hung old pants with cotton wool lining, with their front against my chest and the trouser legs hanging over my shoulders. They were going to protect me from the sharp steel posts and razor sharp wires which would have cut into my hands and stomach and perhaps forced me to remain stuck atop the fence...

I took two steps forward, rested one end of the ladder against the ground and the other—against the top of the fence. The top of the ladder reached above the steel post! Ten steps up the ladder, moving like a scalded cat! The pants covered the post and the wire. I lay on my stomach, rolled over the obstacle and fell ten feet to the ground. Fate was kind to me and I fell on my feet into a puddle of semi-liquid excreta, which found their way from the latrine to the other side of the fence. However, my escape caused the rusty barbed wire to make a hideous noise, which caused all sentries to instantly wake up. It was dark and they could not fathom out what was going on. Instead of the standard command: "Stop or I'll shoot!"– we heard something which sounded like: "What's going on? Where!?" Followed by a pow!–pow!– pow! roughly in my direction, but with the shots aimed above the invisible target, so as not to hit an adjacent tower. Phew-phew-phew went above my head the sharp-ended bullets from the guards' rifles.

Crash–stomp–crash went the escapees who were either jumping or falling over the fence. Luckily, nobody was injured in that mad scramble.

"Go!"–went the command –and the herd stampeded over the vegetable gardens, jumping over the vegetable patches and the low fences separating individual holdings –over the first, the second–the tenth.. All I could hear behind me were heavy breathing, curses and profanities.

We reached a road by the time we reached the outskirts of a small miners' settlement. The dawn was breaking but the settlement looked empty. We stopped running, quickly walking instead, and discussing the situation, when a woman suddenly appeared on the low porch of a home. Our chatter was at once replaced by a stunned silence. Silent was also the woman. I can't tell to this day whether she understood who were the members of the rag-tag mob leaving the settlement and decided, thank God, not to give us away, or whether she had no idea who we might have been...

Having finally reached the outskirts of the village I told my companions to head for a nearby swamp as I was expecting a pursuit with the use of dogs, who have trouble picking up scent in a wet environment.

Our group must have looked quite intimidating. All of us were dressed in torn clothing, with crumpled hats and caps on our heads and worn out shoes on our feet. I was the only one to sport an old suede jacket hailing all the way from Harbin, which at one point in my imprisonment I had to wrestle out of the clutches of a crim who wanted to confiscate it. One pocket of that jacket contained a flat tin filled with salt and the other—an identical container with makhorka (*inferior tobacco—MH*).

We marched in a long row. The small agile Volodka was keeping close to me, with the others lagging behind. An hour passed by and the sun was getting quite hot. I kept up a brisk pace so as to increase the distance between us and the camp and to quickly reach a forest, which I could see on the hills beyond the swamp. That unfortunately meant that the gap between me and the rest of the group kept increasing leading to angry shouts of: "Listen, you bloody hunter! You are used to running like a trotter, but this pace is not for us! Stop! Have a break!" I snapped and told them to stop whinging, but had to give in and organise a rest break in the end, but not before we reached the forest.

Volodya and I continued to guide the escapees following a rest, avoiding roads and paths and carefully walking around small cottages whose vegetable gardens were located on small meadows in the middle of the forest.

Coming to the end of a field we suddenly heard the unmistakable "ga-ga-ga" sound made by domestic geese and spotted three of them running into the bushes. The nimble Ryazanoff jumped for them like a lynx, grabbed one of them by the neck and disappeared into the bushes, and at that very moment I spotted a bucket with cut up potatoes ready for planting. One leap—grab—and we are running through the scrub with the goose flapping its wings in sheer desperation. A short stop, a twist of the goose's neck and a continuation of our run! The mad rush continues until the sun is high in the sky when we find a small brook, collapse on the ground and slowly regain our senses. The rest of the group slowly joins us. We start a smokeless fire using dry twigs and make a goose soup with fresh potatoes! For the first time in months we get a fill of such an incredibly tasty thick soup. The meal over, we collapse on the grass and have a two-hour sleep. We do not hear any sounds of men or dogs, but a suspicious small plane keeps circling over the forest. Looking for us? We lie motionless hiding under the crowns of young oak trees.

We continue our way north along a low mountain ridge overgrown with scraggy oak trees; to the right of us we see tilled fields and on the left—the floodplains of the Suifoon River, which flows into the Gulf of Amur near the settlement of Tavrichanka. The well-trained eyes of professional thieves belonging to my mates noticed all of a sudden a small chicken farm in at the bottom of a gully. This led to a plan of a raid. I was left behind as a look-out and the professionals sneaked up through the bushes to the farm. The mission was successfully accomplished, with the raiders returning after nightfall carrying bags with thirteen chickens!

In the morning we dug up some seed potatoes cut into small pieces (this was another sign of the famine ravaging the land in 1947) and made some chicken soup sitting in an aider-tree grove nestled in the flood plains of the Suifoon River.

At nightfall I managed to talk my companions into going to the shores of the Suifoon, as I was long aware that we must cross to its eastern bank, cross a plain and head for the Blue Ridge hills on the border with Manchuria. That was our only hope of escape from Russia.

Upon reaching the Suifoon I found what I was looking for: the only ford in the area marked by a rut made by the wheels of numerous horse-driven carts. It was obvious that it led to the other side of the stream and that it was shallow enough for use by a grown man. We would, get wet, of course, but that was unimportant as we could start a fire and get dry and warm.

Having picked a suitable spot I stepped into the water and noticed that the water not overly cold, and, in any event, would it matter even if it was? The bottom of the river was firm and the current quite slow. I shouted: "Follow me!" and kept walking for another thirty-odd paces, noticing that the water barely reached my waist. I turned around to see how the rest of our company were faring and could not believe my eyes: that mob were milling around on the shore without making a move into the water.

"Come on, Volodya!"–I shouted, sure that he would not let me down. I was halfway across the river, with only a few of its equally shallow arms remaining to be crossed -no problem at all! But....the crims started to scream:

"Come back! We can't swim! You have two of our chickens left in your bag and you gave your word not to abandon us!" The worst thing was that Volodya joined in the chorus...

"Should I go on and let them go to hell?"–thought I. The other shore was near and so were the mountains. It was obvious that the searchers chose another direction. I would reach the mountains by the morning and could conceivably cross the border ridge later in the day. However, did I have the right to abandon my mates? After all, we all swore to stick to each other in case of trouble. What was I to do?

"Come back"–continued the screams–"let's keep going till we find a boat and cross safely! Don't forget—you gave your word!"...

"Word"–that's what forced me to turn around. That's how I was brought up. Little did I know at the time the value of their "words!" I made my way back to the eastern shore and reached it with the water never rising above my waist. That was my first mistake, my first quarrel, the first betrayal on the part of Vladimir Rozanoff, the man with whom I was inseparable from Pyongyang and who seemed to be such a resolute and trustworthy friend.

CHAPTER 2

From that moment on our group split into two unequal parts with different aims: I on the one side, and the remaining four on the other. I wanted to keep surging ahead, whereas all they wanted was to stick around awaiting nebulous "better times". Some of them saw themselves in "jumping onto a freight train and getting to some far-away places", and others in "finding a job in an apiary."—all preposterous notions, based on the assumption that our jailers were going to forget about us. The worst thing about it all was that Rozanoff was on the side of that unprincipled rabble! He underwent an instant metamorphosis.

Our clothing and equipment were positively outlandish. Volodya and I got hold of some tailors' scissors in the camp, pulled them apart and converted them into two "knives" which we wore behind our belts. I had metal boxes with matches, salt and makhorka (rough tobacco). I also picked up an axe during our days on the run and carried it in a sling over my shoulder. Vaska Krivonos found a scythe and was also carrying this over his shoulder. All in all our rag-tag mob, which was frightened of every roadside bush, was reminiscent of a gang of labourers or bandits, and behaved like the latter. Former petty thieves from a homeless background raided every convenient empty yard or barn in order to grab anything that they could lay their hands on, such as rags, bits of iron and barely edible bran. However, they never found any bread, as absolutely none was available in that spring.

I tried to reason with them, explaining that we were leaving behind clues for our pursuers, but all was in vain: they were the majority and had no intention of listening to the opinion of an outsider. The refusal of those cowards to ford Suifoon meant that we had to keep walking along its left bank in the hope of finding a boat or of reaching an observation post called Razdolnoye and trying to cross the bridge adjacent to it, provided it was not being guarded.

Thus stupidly and senselessly we lost three days, fitfully sleeping on the ground, getting wet in the rain and consuming all our chickens. We again reached the shores of Suifoon at the end of the third day, this time near Razdolnoye and found two boats, which were moored to the shore with substantial rusty chains and large locks. It took us an hour to break the first lock, using stones for that purpose. The boat sunk immediately after we finally pushed it into the water and jumped into it, as it had developed huge cracks from staying on the shore for a long time, and fountains of water were rushing into it. We barely managed to escape from it, left it to its own devices and started on the second one, whose lock yielded much quicker, jumped into it and took off using our hands and a board instead of the ores. The current was strong, but we managed to get to the other shore, which turned out to be an island! Having disembarked, we abandoned the boat and hid in the thick bushes of weeping willow where, cold and miserable, we managed to have some sleep till dawn.

Vaska noticed two fishermen at early dawn, who moored their boat and walked away, evidently to their favourite fishing spot. We crept up to the boat, cut off the connecting rope and soon managed to get to the western shore of the Suifoon. I can only imagine the "delight" of the fishermen when they came back!

CHAPTER 2

I knew that in order to get away from the cluster of roads and settlements we had to cross the highway and the railway which lead from Razdolnoye to the towns of Kraskino and Khasan and continue to the Korean border. Beyond them lie hills and ridges, which terminate at a watershed provided by the Blue (*"Sinij" in Russian MH*) Ridge, which also forms the border between Russia and Manchuria. That was the shortest way to freedom, the aim of our venture. I considered that we could go without food for a day or two in order to achieve our aim, keeping in mind that there was every chance of catching some fish or boiling some edible roots of the so-called "devil's tree" and, if the worse came to the worst, eating frogs. I used to eat fried frogs in my day. The answer to my suggestion was: "It's OK for you, you bloody taiga (*Siberian Forest–MH*) dweller, you! You can even thrive on snakes, but we don't agree with your ideas! We are going to help ourselves to a piglet in the first village we come to!"

The village, whose name was Nezjino, came into our view after we crossed the highway. I was again adjudged unsuitable for a raid and was left behind in the bushes, with the petty crims walking off in search of a meal. However, less than an hour later I heard the barking of the dogs accompanied by horrifying screams and saw the silly band running for their lives in my direction. Barely being able to catch their breath, they related a plaintive tale of a failed robbery. It seems that they got hold of a large piglet, but were first attacked by a dog, followed by a mob of peasant women, with a group of farmers running towards the crooks from some distance away. I am unable to this day to fathom out why they did not continue their pursuit, as we would have had little chance of outrunning them. However, they must have turned back and we were able to continue westward along the highway, crossing it first, followed by the railway line. Panting and puffing we climbed the first hillock, found a small meadow and collapsed on the ground.

The sun was getting quite hot and I looked around me. It was a marvellous morning in the beginning of June. The trees and shrubs were in full bloom, bright young grass was everywhere, and the soil was full of fragrance of Spring. A pheasant was calling higher up in the mountains. Would I be able to entice it to come closer and to kill it with a stick? Or what were my chances of finding its nest full of eggs? I got up and started climbing towards the top of the ridge. I reached a peak from which I could see the vista of the whole of the Blue Ridge. Our hillock was part of a smaller ridge, which was undulating upwards towards the blue sky and stopped at the Blue Ridge somewhere near the horizon. It was covered in light green broadleaved trees, which were replaced by dark conifers at greater heights. They would provide a secure cover from the small plane which we kept seeing circling the area at a low height -a sure sign that our jailers were looking for us.

I was enchanted by the sight of the Blue Ridge. How far was it? Twenty, or perhaps, at most, thirty kilometres? If we were to step on it, we could reach it by nightfall. All we had to do was to lie low near the border and find out the timing of the border patrols. Then it was very easy indeed to jump over the forest cutting marking the border—and be gone! Should a bullet end one's life at that point—well, that's fate...Will

I manage to break through, get to see the eyes of my wife and to hold my first-born child?

For the first time in days I was alone with my thoughts. I did not have to run, to listen to complaints and to look at revolting mugs of creatures who held nothing sacred and who only aim in life was to steal, to fill their gobs and to sit idly tight...

As far as I was concerned, that shiny morning, the blue forest and hills were the embodiment of happiness, a wonderful fairytale. Be that time long or short, I was free and could walk wherever I pleased, breathe the scent of fresh grass and flowers, see the mountains, forests, meadows and streams. All that was alive and familiar to me since childhood. What happiness! The only thing that was missing was at least one kindred soul by my side. What should I do? Should I abandon that scum and keep walking westwards through the taiga (*Siberian forest MH*), my beloved taiga, which should guide me to salvation, and if not, it is infinitely preferable to die here than in a malodorous prison.

These were my thoughts, whereas my legs kept taking me to the gully where I left my "mates".

I kept trying to lure the pheasant cock who was still in the vicinity, by imitating the cry of a hen, but was unable to get him although he did come quite close. I returned to my sleeping companions who reminded me from a distance of a herd of sleeping wild pigs and at close range turned out to be a heap of dirty jackets worn by sleepy muttering ruffians.

I stopped and agonised once more. If I leave these traitors to their own devices, I will most certainly escape, but if I stay, they will betray me at a drop of a hat. But...I did promise not to leave them under any circumstances, curse it, and how would I feel for the rest of my life if I betrayed them?

I took a deep breath and woke up that cursing crew and led it to a rocky peak from which we had a view of all our surroundings. We saw several gullies, with a village in each of them. To the left was a hamlet where steers, heifers and cows were grazing in a large enclosure, and a flock of sheep was grazing on a meadow to our right, under the watchful eye of a shepherd.

That scene destroyed all my plans. My charges eyed me with an open hatred. "We are not going anywhere until we catch a calf. We are going to sit here till the evening, get the beast, slaughter and cook it, fill our bellies and then go..."

It was, alas, impossible to prevail under those circumstances. Life has its laws and a man can sometimes find himself in a situation where he feels that he is imprisoned in a kind of an invisible whirlpool without a chance of escape...

We waited till nightfall and a man called Krivonos, a big awkward lad called Vovka and I went towards the village, leaving the rest behind. It was dark, but we were spotted by some farmers who wanted to know who we were, to which we responded with an unconvincing tale, and took a roundabout route to the barn. Several beasts were wandering about in the enclosure and we waited for a calf to leave it, but had no success. After two futile hours had passed, Vovka decided to see what else could be done, went towards the village and disappeared. We heard voices at first, followed by complete silence. Having waited till dawn, we went back to our camp in the hope that he managed to find his way there, but he was not there either, which made us think that he had been captured. It was imperative to keep going, but Rozanoff and Ivan stated that they were sick, had no strength left and would not move until we caught at least a sheep.

The sun had risen by that time and we began to wonder whether Vovka was not asleep somewhere and would turn up after all. A flock of sheep appeared from the village to our right accompanied by a shepherd. The "patients" staged an immediate recovery: "Let's catch a sheep and be gone!"

My heart was not in that enterprise, but I joined them nevertheless. This time there were only Vaska and I. By that time the herd had moved from the meadow to our side of the hill and we started to follow it through the forest. There they were—closer, ever closer. The shepherd's well-worn jumper could be clearly seen through the scrub, with the man himself sitting on a fallen log and absent-mindedly looking at the ground. He raised his head when he saw us approaching him.

"Where are you from lads?" –asked he in an alarmed voice.

The old man was about seventy and had a scraggy white beard, discoloured by a continuous use of tobacco. An old cap sat on his head; he was dressed in a torn coat; an old rubber boot was on one of his feet, with a torn shoe on the other. About three dozen sheep were quietly grazing a few feet away.

We kept slowly walking towards him with a feverish thought going through my mind: "How should we introduce ourselves so as not to arouse his suspicion?"–as our appearance was far from reassuring. We had not shaved for a few days, our clothes were torn, baggy and covered in soot after our wanderings and nights spent at the campfire. I was carrying an axe over my shoulder and used it to misrepresent our background.

"We are enlisted fishermen on the Suifoon River and are cutting down some poles for a hut. Don't worry, grandpa, let's have a smoke."

We sat on both sides of the old fellow and I took out a tin with makhorka, provided each of us with a piece of newspaper, and used one of my last matches to light the self-rolled cigarettes.

"And how are you, grandpa? What is your job? Where are you from?"

The shepherd was glad to tell us about himself whilst enjoying his smoke. He had recently moved here from Byelorussia and was employed as a shepherd at the collective farm. Life was bad. "It couldn't be any worse", said he.

We listened to his tales of woe and commiserated with the old fellow but realised that something had to be done, although it was dreadful to harm such an unfortunate man. Krivonos was the first one to bite the bullet.

CHAPTER 2

"We are going to take one of your sheep, grandpa" –said he, putting a hand on his shoulder.

"Please don't do it to me lads!" –begged the old man—"I'll have to go to jail for that!"

Vaska managed to mollify him by saying:

"Don't be afraid! We'll tie you up and won't be accused of anything."

"No-oo"– said the old boy, but Vaska forced him on to the ground, sat on top of the poor chap and started tying up his arms behind his back.

It was shameful indeed for us two strong men to tie up an old defenceless man, but we had no option. I used a piece of rope to tie up his elbows and wrists, with the unfortunate man singing out:

"What are you doing?"

Vaska blew up:

"We are done for if he keeps screaming! We must gag him!"

I took a big red handkerchief out of the poor fellow's pocket, folded it and covered his mouth and the walrus-like tobacco-stained moustache. Grandpa made a gurgling sound when I tied the handkerchief behind his head and I made sure that the gag was not too tight.

"Not too tight? Can you breathe?"

"Yeah..."

Looking around I could not help laughing despite the drama of the situation when I saw Vaska tying up grandpa's legs with a rope and using a thin cord to attach it to a tiny shrub! He was anchoring our unfortunate victim!

"Leave it! He will not get anywhere! Let's catch a sheep!"

We got up from the ground and looked around, but the sheep, which had been quietly grazing to that moment, became restless and started heading for the hills. We walked talking quietly to each other about forty metres behind the animals, realising that they were heading for the peak where Volodya Ryazanoff and Ivan were waiting for us. Things were working out well. We only had about one kilometre to go and could see the rocks through a light fog. The sheep were heading for a trap, when all of a sudden we heard the "ta-ta-ta" of submachine guns coming from our camp and saw small dark figures darting about!

Vaska froze.

"Our mates are trapped! Let's run!"

At that very moment the frightened mob of sheep turned around and ran towards us. I yanked the axe off my shoulder and hit a young seep over the head, killing it instantly.

"Leave it, let's run!"– screamed panic-stricken Vaska.

"No way, mate, I am not going to run without it", said I and slung the beast over my shoulder before we made a rapid dash across the meadow into a gully overgrown with alder trees, covering the 200 metres to that area with the speed of racehorses. We tumbled into the ravine, scampered to a brook and laid still, looking at small figures of men which could be seen through the thick foliage at the top of the hill and listening to the sounds of instructions barked by their officers.

However, silence fell after some time and the bright light of day was replaced by dusk.

I gutted the sheep with my makeshift knife made out of one half of a pair of scissors, drank some of its blood, gave some to Vaska Krivonos and taught him to eat the raw liver, which still retained some of its warmth.

We skinned the sheep burying its skin and head and putting the meat into a bag. There was not much meat, but it could last us for a couple of days. At nightfall I, followed by Vaska, started walking through the forest towards the top of the ridge. Having found a small flat area in the thick undergrowth, which hid us from observers, we settled in a cosy spot under a fallen cedar tree and made a smokeless fire on which we cooked a few kebabs. The meal over, we crawled under its thick trunk and were soon asleep.

I woke up at dawn; Vaska was still peacefully asleep. I crawled out of our nest and took a few deep breaths of the fresh spring air, which reminded me of many happy days of hunting expeditions in the Korean and Manchurian taiga (*forest MH*). Can it be that I'll be there tomorrow? To be sure, many obstacles had yet to be overcome, such as hundreds of kilometres of taiga and encounters with new people. What will they be like? What will be their attitude towards me? The future was foggy but the main thing was to get away from our pursuers and to get rid of the feeling of being like a wild animal, who was a fair game for anybody's bullet.

It was a fine morning of the fifth of June 1947. We had to go without delay. I tapped Vaska on the shoulder.

"Get up!"—said I.

"M-mm"—was an indistinct reply.

Having called him once more and received an indistinct response along the lines that there was plenty of time yet, followed by my mate turning over onto his belly, I said:

"Well, then sleep till they pick you up!"

I realised that his conduct freed me from all my promises, that I was free from them at last. I divided up the pieces of meat and the remaining 8 matches, making it 4 each, and got up ready to leave, when Vaska crawled out of the nest with a yawn, saying :

"OK. Let's go"...

Later I often thought that there were three defining moments in that adventure, each of which would have brought me success. The first one was when I turned around in the middle of the Suifoon River and returned to my companions. The second one—when I saw that lot sleeping like a herd of wild pigs, and this moment was the third. Had I in each of these moments acted in accordance with common sense instead of a chivalrous instinct of a Don Quixote, I would have abandoned my companions and gone it alone.

Where would I have been now? I have no doubt whatsoever that I would have reached the border with a grassless strip tens of metres wide and an adjacent path along which twice or three times a day walk border guards and their dogs on their way between observation posts located five kilometres apart. It is not hard to dash across that strip, provided one can miss a patrol or a high voltage wire. It is harder to do so without leaving any traces, but it is doubtful if the guards were allowed to cross the border in pursuit of a fugitive. Yes, but what if they are? Well, I would have just taken that risk and accepted it as part of life of a man on the run..

Putting aside my thoughts, I put the matches back into my box, as they had been mine in the first place. None of my companions thought of taking along some matches and salt, and I was also a fortunate owner of an axe by now.

We reached a small narrow hilltop, which led directly to the Blue Ridge and it was imperative for us to follow it in order to avoid our pursuers. However, Vaska started whingeing that we did not have enough food for such a long trip and wanted to find a potato field in order to get some extra provisions. At that moment we saw a recently tilled field and started walking towards it. I was concerned about the clumsiness of that petty thief and told him to sit tight while I went to look for a safe way of accessing the field. He was nowhere to be seen after I returned from my reconnaissance, but suddenly I heard a whistle and saw the blighter in a nearby gully ravaging a small apiary. He had taken the lid off one of the bee hives and was waging a desperate war with the bees. I rushed down and confronted him:

"What the hell are you doing, you idiot? Let's go!"

"Rubbish!"—was the reply—"let's each take a frame of honeycombs and to hell with the potatoes!"

Stupid though that statement was, there was some modicum of logic in it.

"OK, but let's push the hive into the brook to stop being attacked."

We overturned the hive into the cold water causing the bees to flee and each got hold of a frame of honeycomb containing a fair bit of honey. Vaska looked revolting; he was devouring honey together with the wax and drones, some of whom had stayed behind. We were wet to the waist and had to at least squeeze out some water to make walking easier. We walked for about two hundred metres, took off our shoes and started to dry off. I instinctively felt that I had made a fatal mistake when I allowed that primitive and senseless oaf to push me around...

"Did you see anybody near the apiary?"—I asked.

"Yeah, a farmer was walking with a cow nearby, but I don't think he saw me."

"What do you mean, you fool? Do you think he was stupid enough to shout at you? He would have informed the authorities after returning to the village!"

"No, he did not see me!"

The end of our gully was covered in fog, but I noticed a movement at that spot. At first it looked as if a young shepherd was driving a calf with a stick, which meant that we had to wait for him to pass before running towards the forest. It was a nuisance but certainly no catastrophe. I whispered a command to Vaska and we sat down behind sparse shrubs, but I immediately realised that I was mistaken, as it was a soldier leading a German shepherd on a leash. A second soldier appeared from the fog and our only hope was that they would walk past our hiding place as it was separated from them by a brook, some shrubs and a total distance of about thirty metres.

"Lie down", –commanded I and we fell flat on to the ground. The soldiers were getting closer but did not see us as they were looking straight ahead. A few more paces, and we could make a run for it. If the dog was to catch up with me, I was going to kill it with my axe. There was no way they were going to capture me in the forest. My mate Vaska would have also had to learn to run like a deer...

The procession nearly passed us when the dog turned its head in our direction. It could not pick up our scent as the wind was blowing towards us, but its master automatically looked in our direction and saw two semi-naked figures crouching on the ground.

"Here they are! Hands up! Don't move!"–followed by the "rat-tat-tat" of two semi-automatic guns. Bullets were knocking down branches above our heads and grey smoke from the weapons was rising above the heads of the soldiers. I think that they were not aiming at us and I suddenly realised that they had run out of ammunition. Rapidly rising to my feet, I was about to jump into the thicket without considering the consequences of my action, when I suddenly noticed five more men armed with submachine guns who were approaching me from the back. That was it! I was about to be cut in half by their bullets. I sat down, slowly rolling over to one side and remember my thought: "The fairytale is over."

And what of Vaska? The "heroic" professional thief (he always bragged about his bravery) was lying on his back, arms and legs in the air, shouting:

"Don't shoot! I am lying down!"

Minutes later we were driven like cattle. The soldiers were cursing loudly:

"You scum! You reptiles! Because of you, dirty dogs, we had to feed mosquitoes for a whole week, hardly slept and went hungry...".

Then suddenly—bash! I thought that a heavy sledge hammer hit me in the left ear, but it was a butt of an automatic rifle. I collapsed and instinctively grabbed hold of my ear, which suddenly swelled in my palm to the size of a large mushroom.

"Stop it! Don't you dare touch him!"–barked one of the officers.

"Get up, they won't hit you again"—said he to me.

I got up with great difficulty and walked to a truck, whereupon my mate and I were dragged into it, handcuffed and thrown on the floor of the vehicle. Several sub-machine gunners sat in the corners of its body and the truck travelled along the road full of potholes towards the collective farm from which we tried to steal some cattle two days ago.

The farm office had been converted into the search headquarters. A colonel sat at a telephone and was shouting into it as we were placed into a corner:

"We caught them, comrade general! Yes, yes, and their ataman (*leader–MH*) –the White bandit! Aye- aye—aye!"

CHAPTER 2

A captain walked up to him and whispered in his ear. The colonel put down the receiver and looked at us:

"Take them outside, let the farmers look at them and say a few words. Hands behind the back—and on the porch" – said he to us.

I stepped outside through an open door and saw a yard full of people. Men, women, kids. The crowd was pushing towards the steps towards my manacled figure. Somebody shouted:

"There he is, the ataman of the criminals! Look at him! It was he who stole the sheep and tied up the old shepherd!"

The crowd was getting closer. Some of them were armed with sticks and pitchforks.

"What did you bash up the grandpop for? He is sick with fever now! You scum! You ought to be killed!"…

I realised that I was about to be stabbed and hit over the head with a stick and replied as calmly and as loudly as I could:

"I did not touch the grandpa. On the contrary, I gave him a smoke. Yes, we took the sheep, but when I tied him up and gagged him, I made sure that he could breathe easily." …

The officer standing behind me realised that the mob was likely to lynch me and shouted:

"OK, you've seen him, and that's enough. He is going back into the office now!"

I sighed with relief. No matter how bad things were going to be, lynch law was not going to be used.

The colonel greeted my return with a statement:

"You are very lucky indeed that capital punishment was abolished yesterday. You would have been shot if it was not for that"..

Following that interlude, we were again being transported like logs on the floor of the truck, which was rocking and rolling over the potholes, and finally stopped outside the counterintelligence headquarters of the Razdolnoye village, where three days earlier we were breaking locks and stealing boats.

Two submachine-gunners pushed me into the investigator's office and stood behind me. I stood holding up my trousers, which had no buttons or belt facing a small fat curly-haired and red faced major sitting behind a desk holding a TT pistol in his hand. He jumped up and pointed it at me.

"Lie down!" screeched he.

I could see that he was panic stricken at the sight of me. He was scared that the bandit standing in front of him would jump over the desk and strangle him. Even the soldiers standing behind my back were unable to guarantee that he would not lose his precious life... I sat down near the threshold. He hit the table with the handle of his pistol and screamed at the top of his voice:

"Lie down!!!"

That red-haired dwarf was a coward. He must have spent the whole war fighting unarmed prisoners.

I swear, that I felt like laughing. I lay down, put one hand under my head and asked:

"Will that do?"

CHAPTER 2

"Don't talk! I ask questions here!"

"I am not going to talk until you give me something to eat", said I calmly.

The major gave in and let me have a bowl of barley porridge, which to me tasted like a meal fit for the gods. I answered his preliminary questions and was led to a cell where I crawled between the hot bodies of its inmates and immediately fell into a deep sleep...

Chapter 3: The Remand Prison

I was very fortunate to have been saved further encounters with the psychopathic major. The following morning we were again put into the truck, which took us to the remand (high-security) prison in Ussuriysk, where we were placed in separate cells. My cell was the last one on the left in the prison hallway and I had a good look at my new companions after its door shut behind me with the accompanying squeak of its lock. The most prominent of them was a middle-aged but strong Japanese sporting a grey carefully clipped drooping moustache. The samurai introduced himself as a retired major general Hasebe, the commander of the first brigade to enter Harbin during the occupation of Manchuria in 1931.

The second one was a major of the Chiang Kai Shek Army who was youthful, clean shaven and yellow faced. My third companion was a Russian, a Red Army lieutenant by the name of Kovalev who fought in the Russo-Finnish War, had been imprisoned by the Finns and subsequently fought in the War against Germany right to its end. However, SMERSH had not forgotten his imprisonment and wanted to find out whether he had been recruited by the enemy. Kovalev's interrogation had already lasted for sixteen months and he was nervous, hungry and utterly demoralised. He would cry at the drop of a hat and had lost all willpower. He was unable to wait for the nine grams of sugar, which followed the morning issue of a small piece of soggy black bread and would cry and immediately swallow the bread...

Hasabe spoke excellent though slightly accented Russian and the Chinese major spoke passable Japanese and I was therefore able to engage them in conversations on any chosen topic, but Kovalev had no common language with the Chinaman and hated him, being sure that the latter was a stooge who was being given secret extra rations. He based his suspicion on the fact that the major drank a lot of water, which, in Kovalev's opinion, was a sure sign of a well-fed person. On my first day in that cell he attacked the Chinaman with the lid of the toilet bowl and I, though a new inmate, was forced to give the poor nut a clip over the ear and to forcibly seat him in a corner.

Our cell was a low room about three metres long and four metres wide. Low bunks were located along its length with a chamber pot sitting in one of its corners. The entrance door contained a hole for the observation of the interior and a small second door through which we were given food.

We were not allowed to sleep during the day, having to sit down instead. The energetic Hasabe used to walk the four metres to and fro one thousand times a day, making it a total of four kilometres. He would also, despite his 68 years, strip to his underwear during morning ablutions, pour cold water over his torso and vigorously dry himself off, till his skin was showing a red glow.

After breakfast we were given a twenty minute walk in the small yard of our prison. We had to follow each other in a circle, with hands behind our backs. I noticed that the barbed wire fence surrounding our yard was overgrown with a pinkish–green weed called goose-food ("lebeda" in Russian). I would pick a moment when the sentry would look another way, tear off a few leaves of lebeda, hide them under my shirt, cut them up into small pieces upon return to the cell and use them as a garnish for the prison broth I received for lunch. I am not sure about the nutrition value of that weed but I did derive a fair amount of satisfaction from the feeling of fullness produced by the garnish. My mates noticed my antics and started to follow my example and thus unofficially increase their rations, but the clumsy Kovalev got caught in the act. We were all roared up and the collection of lebeda was forbidden forthwith. That, however, did not stop us from thus supplementing our rations whenever we could get away with it.

Lunch was handed out by a young buxom lass by the name of Mashka. It seemed that she was supplementing her own rations with the food she withheld from the prisoners. The procedure was the same every lunchtime: the small door in the entrance door would be opened and Mashka's pink arm would appear in the opening bearing a half-litre scoop filled with food. We stood in a queue and would each produce our bowl in turn, to have our rations poured into it. I found that arm disturbing and told my mates that I was going to tear it off one day.

I said so in Russian and Japanese keeping a poker face, which produced a polite grin from the Asians, but caused Kovalev to burst into tears, because he thought that I was serious. However, Kovalev's tears notwithstanding, I was deeply resentful of Mashka because she was obviously growing fat as a result of stealing our food...

We were fortunate in that we were allowed to talk during the day and we used that good fortune in full measure. We talked about the past, but mostly about our current preoccupation with food. Poor Kovalev used to get upset and cry because we had to use Japanese which he did not know. Our reminiscences concerned most sophisticated dishes. "I'll never stop eating if I ever get out of here..." would we all say.

General Hasabe had lived a long and interesting life and was an excellent storyteller. During the First World War he served as a young seconded captain of the Japanese Imperial at the headquarters of the Russian Emperor Nicholas the Second and was often invited to share his meals with the Royal family. He remembered that the Tsar wore the uniform of an Army colonel made of heavy grey cloth and was always very polite and easy to talk to.

He also remembered a funny story. It seems that already in Soviet times he was travelling from Tokyo to Moscow. In the port city of Dairen they boarded a train, which was to take them to their destination via Manchuria. The passengers would leave their shoes outside the doors of their cabins at night and collect them in the morning after they had been beautifully polished by the service staff.

CHAPTER 3

All went well until they reached the Otpor Station on the border with Russia. "That evening"—remembered general Hasabe with a laugh—"I kept my shoes in the cabin knowing that a Russian crew was going to take over from the Japanese". He said nothing about it to his companions. When the morning came, one of the diplomats repaired for the toilet and was surprised that his shoes were not in their usual place. The same fate befell the other travellers of that carriage. They were unable to buy replacements and appeared on the Moscow Railway Station wearing torn slippers provided by the sheepish Chief Conductor, but not Hasabe, who proudly sported his uncleaned leather shoes.

Hasabe's best story concerned his visits to Paris when the young diplomat was taken to an establishment called "The Beauty Salon", where the visitors took off their clothes, had a shower and walked along a long carpeted corridor until they entered a dark hall through a narrow secret door. Soft music was playing and naked bodies were entwined in a voluptuous dance. People were sitting, walking around, embracing and kissing. Everything was done by touch and participants communicated in whispers in all the languages of the world. There were two exit doors—one for each sex, and anybody could leave at any time. The doors led to the hallway, the shower and the dressing room where one got dressed and walked out into an empty street within a couple of paces from the entrance to the modern-day European Babylon.

The old general was quite moved by those memories and concluded them with a story of a visit to a very expensive cabaret where the visitors were being served by "live statues". They were waitresses, who were made up to look like marble statues and "I could swear that they were real statues until one of them would move towards a customer and take his order. They were so beautiful that I could not take my eyes off them"-- he said.

One evening we were remembering life before our imprisonment, things we did at home, parties we attended and clothes we wore. I said smilingly:

"I left twelve suits at home: two dinner-suits, three light woollen ones, three summer suits and a couple of sporting outfits."...

Our chat was interrupted by the click of the opening of a peephole in the cell door followed by the appearance of a grey eye in the opening .We fell silent and heard the creak of a key in the door, whereupon the door opened and the emaciated figure of one of our prison guards appeared on the threshold. He stuck his head into the cell and hissed:

"Twelve suits, indeed...Give us a break! Tell lies by all means, but make sure that they are at least plausible!" The door closed and the apparition vanished...

We exchanged meaningful glances: it was obvious that the poor fellow was unlikely to possess even one decent suit.

The investigation lasted till August. I was often transported to my interrogations in a prison wagon camouflaged as a food delivery van, with the word "BREAD" written on its side. That was a real torture, as the prisoners were crammed into boxes where one could neither sit nor stand. And had to contort oneself into the shape of a question mark, which meant trying to seek support by alternately pushing against the walls, with the head, back and knees. The journey, which involved a rock and roll over innumerable pot-holes, seemed to last an eternity, and it was dark, dusty and stuffy.

There was one redeeming feature, however: my investigator by the name of captain Shevchenko turned out to be a remarkably humane and just person. I shall never forget him. It has to be said that I was not trying to pull the wool over his eyes and told him an absolute truth. And, in any event, what was the point in telling fibs? I told him exactly what happened to the point of the Ukrainian commandant of the camp replying to my complaint about the threatening behaviour of some prisoners with: "The sheep get used to their surroundings after a few butting episodes." I told Shevchenko that I was not guilty of any crimes and for that reason decided to escape to Manchuria, where my wife, son and relatives were waiting for me. Rozanoff and I were going to try to escape on our own, but the other three were chance companions and we never invited them to join us....

My interrogator's companions would often pop into his office during the interrogation. They looked at me with complete indifference treating me as a piece of furniture ignoring my appearance of an emaciated prisoner with closely cropped hair. They talked about their everyday affairs, joked and laughed. I could not imagine myself engaging in such a light-hearted banter in the presence of a condemned man.

Chapter 3

Meanwhile the captain was listening attentively to my story and wrote it down without any alterations or additions, which happens sometimes under those circumstances. I felt that he understood my plight and even felt sorry for me. He allowed me to smoke and even gave me some cigarettes to take to my cell. He even once gave me a sandwich with red caviar. He said once:

"I like you and I feel that you are telling me the truth. However, your pals are all scum. They are trying to blame you for everything and think that that is going to help them, but it won't. It is not something that is a normal procedure, but I can show you their testimony if you are interested. Do you want to see it?"

He did show me their evidence, in which my "mates" unanimously blamed me, insisting that I talked them into fleeing to Manchuria, promising them mountains of gold for their help. The worst thing, though, was the fact that Volodya Rozanoff, whom I regarded as a friend, joined the others in their lies. I did not expect such a low act from him.

"Have you read it? I don't trust that riff-raff. You should not have got mixed up with them. Anyway, you can tell your story during the trial and in the meantime I shall write my conclusion."

Hasabe was the first one to be tried. The self-confident general kept saying that he just had to be acquitted. He was a military man who followed orders, did not spy and did not take part in sabotage activities. Being nearly seventy, why could he be expected to be imprisoned for a further length of time?

He went to trial carrying his personal belongings with him. He self-assuredly carried them in a small bundle, nodded at us and departed in the company of the prison guards. It was a prison rule that nobody returned to their old cell after a trial, but a mistake was made this time and a gaunt Hasabe appeared in our cell in the evening. He threw his bundle of clothes in the corner and sat on it. He looked at us and kept silent for a long time.

"Well, Hasabe-san. Did they acquit you? Tell us all about it!"

The Japanese don't cry when they are upset. They laugh instead. The old man gave us a hard look of his hazel eyes and blurted out:

Ha, they gave me a present of another ten years. This means a guarantee that I'll live till 78! Ha–ha—ha!

Nobody smiled. The door suddenly opened and somebody yelled:

"Hasabe, how did you get here? Come out at once!"

He smiled. "How **did** I get here indeed?" Hasabe got up, picked up his bundle, gave us a farewell nod and left the cell. We have never seen him again.

The trial of our group took place on the 18th of August 1947. Once again, for the third time in three years, there was a table covered in green woollen cloth and a military tribunal consisting of a three-member "troika" and a secretary. There was a real case to answer this time as we caused a lot of trouble.

Life is full of incredible coincidences and the tribunal secretary in Ussurijsk was the same fellow who was its secretary during my first trial in Kanko. He recognised me and when the presiding officer asked a purely formal question as to whether a defence counsel was required, the secretary exclaimed:

"Oh no!.Yankovsky is the last one to need a defence lawyer! I remember his expert personal defence in Kanko only too well!"

I confirmed that I did not need a defence lawyer and the trial commenced...

The verdict was tough indeed: each of us got 25v years in the Gulag in accordance with articles 58/14 and 58/11,which referred to a "group counter-revolutionary sabotage." My mates were given an additional five years of loss of rights, whereas I, being a stateless person, escaped that punishment. In other words, the "ringleader" got the lightest sentence. Could it have been due to help from captain Shevchenko?

It was quite strange, I remembered that I barely managed to crawl to my mug of water when my first sentence of six years was "adjusted" to ten. Then my legs felt as if they had been filled with lead and I could barely walk. I still believed in truth and justice then. But I was certainly not expecting any leniency now, and neither did my companions. I suppose that it was for that reason that when we received our sentence "in the name of The Russian Federation" we all uttered an enlightened giggle. Well, that was the maximum, and so what? It was over and though it was a maximum custodial punishment, it was at least not a death sentence...

After the court case the five of us and some Chinese were transferred to a real prison. My companions, particularly Rozanoff, were not game to look me in the the eye.

Our guard locked us up in the visitors' room and went away to get instructions as to where to locate individual prisoners. That was quite annoying, as he could have done it before our arrival. We sat down on a trestle bed and one of my mates suddenly exclaimed:

"Listen, fellows! I think I can smell some potatoes!"

He raced towards a bench and dragged out from underneath it half a bag of fresh potatoes. My God! I had never seen nor will I ever, I am sure, see anything like it in my life! It seemed that instead of human beings I was surrounded by a herd of grunting and champing pigs, with the Chinese being as bad as the Russians. The potatoes were being devoured by nine barely human individuals who hardly bothered to even scrape off the dirt from their surface. The bag was emptied in a matter of minutes, and when we heard the footsteps of the guard we shoved the remaining potatoes under our shirts and pushed the bag back under the bench.

The rude fellow walked in and screamed:

"Where are the potatoes? Give it back, you scum! There was no way you could have devoured it all! I'll be in trouble if you all get sick from them!"

I think that he was not really worried about us but was annoyed that a scarce commodity had vanished in our stomachs and he continued on top of his voice:

"Come on, let's have the hidden stuff!"

CHAPTER 3

The animal-like humans threw the twenty or so hidden potatoes on the floor, and they made a pitiful noise as they bounced around the floor. The jailer cursed loudly and took us to our allocated cells.

Following that episode we found ourselves in a transit camp near Ussurijsk, where I encountered another group of people who were also planning an escape. As far as my "well educated' fellow-escapees were concerned all of them faked illnesses, which were meant to exempt them from transportation to other camps, instead of which they were sent to a hospital. I had no idea at the time how to fake an illness and learned that craft much later. It turned out that there were many ways to raise one's temperature, create a boil, produce a blood-stained sputum etc.

All of my "pals" were successful in their ruse and we parted our ways, luckily never to see each other again. I did, however, find out about Rozanoff's fate when I was already in Magadan. His tricks did not save him from finishing up in the Kolyma region where he chopped off his left hand in order to avoid hard labour and became an orderly in a prison hut and later started working as a secret informer for the authorities. He got many prisoners in trouble and was killed by them when they discovered his role in their misfortunes...

From Ussurijsk I was transferred to a prison on the Red River ("*Krasnaya Rechka*" *in Russian MH*) near Khabarovsk, where I again found myself in international company, this time sharing my cell with two Koreans and a middle-aged Japanese by the name of Kabata. He had been taken as a prisoner of war whilst serving in the Japanese

Guang Dong Army, but an alert Secret Service man established that Kabata had been a member of the Gendarmerie *(Japanese Secret Police MH)*, which "earned" him seven years in the Gulag. He was awaiting transportation to the North and told us about his work in the government—run farms in Siberia. He was enormously impressed with the fertility and the enormous size of its farmlands, but could not fathom out the reason for the Russians' profligate attitude towards its riches. He said in his fluent Russian:

"Oh my, what potato there! Like my fist! A lot, a lot. I dig, I collect, but the overseer he shout: 'Why you slow?'" I say: "Very good potato, I collect the lot." But he say: "Don't worry about potato, you must give hectare, area! Hurry forward!"

"Oh my, oh my! Such good potato all leave on the field! Why hectare?"

The stocky dark-haired fellow with an almost black suntan acquired in the Siberian winds, mournfully shook his head, unable to understand the reason for such farming...

One of my middle-aged Korean fellow-prisoners was good at palm reading. He was very friendly to me because of my knowledge of Korean and offered to read my palm. He spent a lot of time gravely looking at me, shook his head and finally uttered:

"Forty years is a very dangerous age for you (I was 36 at the time). You may not survive 40, but if you do, you'll live well past seventy."

I found out that an escape tunnel was being dug from our cell. It was making good progress, but the prisoners were caught and all of the participants, including me as a potential fugitive, were sent to the Vanino Bay via the town of Komsomolsk, which was my first trip in a so-called "Stolypin carriage." (*Stolypin was the Interior Minister under the Tsar, assassinated by the revolutionaries in 1912 MH*). Who said that Stolypin designed "terrible carriages for the transport of prisoners?" In actual fact they were comfortable compartments separated from the carriage hallway by a grille, designed for three people under the Tsar and carrying 18 (!) under the Communists, with six of us on each bunk meant for one person!

Upon arrival in Komsomolsk we were transported across the Amur River on a small boat and I could not keep my eyes from the waters at the mouth of that magnificent river. The saying that the Amur is splendid in any weather is absolutely correct! We reached the town and Vanino, located on a bay of the Tatar Strait, soon after crossing the Amur.

Heaven knows that thousands upon thousands of people went through that bay! Vanino was a strange little town on top of a hill overlooking the Tatar Bay. It was surrounded by a tall timber palisade and resembled an ancient stockaded town. The only difference was that a barbed wire fence sat above the palisade. Inside were a total of five prison camps separated from each other by gates, with each camp having its own security towers. We were divided into groups of five and led into the town through the main gate. A guard greeted me with a strange question:

"Listen, pal, you would not be a racketeer, would you?"

I must have somehow stood out from the grey mass of prisoners, perhaps because I still had my suede jacket brought from Korea, which somehow survived all my misfortunes.

I stayed in Vanino from October to December, during which time there was a continuing stream of arrival and transportation of other prisoners. It was here that I witnessed a conscious act of self-harm by a prisoner. A young criminal nicknamed Kolyma was terrified of transportation to the Far North. It seems that he had already tasted life in the Kolyma region, whence he got his nickname. I stood near a timber log on which he was cutting some kindling wood as part of his duties as the orderly of our hut, when a message was delivered via the camp grapevine: "Transportation tomorrow!" Upon hearing this horrible news, the crim uttered a frightening barrage of obscenities, put his left hand on the block and chopped off four fingers in one fell swoop! The fingers flew into the heap of splinters, but the hand, though changing its colour to a strange blue, did not start bleeding at once. Kolyma emitted an animal-like cry and rushed towards the first aid room, clutching the mutilated hand with the healthy one. It is quite likely that instead of the Far North he was transported by train to an inland Gulag establishment, but they were no better than Kolyma. In any event, he was unwise to trade off Kolyma for becoming an invalid for the rest of his days.

It was not long before I managed to get myself a "job", first as a distributor of the daily soup rations and later in the mortuary. The carrier's job consisted of going to the kitchen where my mate and I picked up a large barrel of soup, threaded a sturdy stick under its arched handle and carried it to all huts in our camp. The distant huts housed the Balts: Latvians, Lithuanians and Estonians. They were blonde, silent, and strangely submissive fellows. It looked as if the camp criminals robbed these uncomplaining men of all their belongings, as they had neither bowls, nor spoons or pots, although all of them were dressed in paramilitary uniforms and wore forage caps on their shaven heads. All they were given was a sliver of moist bread and two scoops of grey slops a day—hardly a ration to ensure a man's long-term survival.

I remember how once when we were crossing a ditch the crosspiece of my mate's hand-made clog broke in half, he fell down and spilled the contents of the barrel. We were aghast at the sight of the food of one hundred prisoners going tom waste, but most horrible of all was the sight of a barely noticeable trace of barley amid the grey liquid at the bottom of the ditch...

The camp saying was: "The kitchen kettle contains all the allowed rations", but I can't help thinking that the kettle had to contain a lot more foodstuffs and the lion's share of nutrients went to the kitchen staff and the criminal elements, who formed a large percentage of the prison population.

Having got the sack as a distributor as a result of the mishap, I immediately insinuated myself into the job of an undertaker, which also gave me some extra rations. Here I found out that the "goners" *(the Russian word for them was "dokhodyagi" MH)*, i.e. prisoners dying of starvation, were dropping like flies. I remember very well that during my three weeks as an undertaker, we had to make thirteen coffins on a "lean" day and the record was nineteen.

We again started to feverishly prepare an escape. There were a lot of us and one night we were sitting in our hut armed with ropes and hooks ready to storm the fence, when we noticed a glow from a cigarette through the opening in the bushes. It was clear that we had been betrayed and that a detachment of sub-machine gunners was waiting for us. Had it not been for that cigarette, none of us would have survived...

The talk of transportation to the North was revived in the unbelievably cold month of December. A commission was at work, whose task it was to select men who still had some meat left on their bones. We had to strip naked and turn, squat and bend. Those passing the examination were being sent into a separate empty hut, where we again had to strip, throw our belongings into a heap and run into another section where, we were told, we were going to be issued with "a complete northern outfit". The order notwithstanding, I and a few other smart lads kept some warm things, which we managed to smuggle past the guards, whereas the naïve ones received outfits which were not fit for the North and which they had to put on their naked bodies. Their clothes consisted of admittedly new but very thin coats and trousers, a pair of foot bindings and ordinary shoes. The poor devils were dreaming of warm clothes and felt boots (*valenki in Russian MH)*, but were told they were adequately equipped for the North! Following that procedure we were herded into the holds of a large motor vessel, one of many "Liberty-type" ships given to Russia by the Allies during the War as part of the "Lend-Lease" program and named "Krasnogvardeyets" (*Red Guard MH)* by the bolsheviks.

By the time of our boarding the ten-ton giant made of welded steel was utterly frozen to the point where all its sides, partitions and floors and ceilings of its holds were covered in shining purple finger-thick frost. Both walls of its huge "cabins" were flanked with three-tiered freshly knocked-up bunks made of raw rough timber, as a result of which it is also covered in ice. I climbed to the top of one bunk with a group of feverishly shaking prisoners. We were trying to get warm with the aid of bits of canvas, which we managed to scrounge up on the way in.

We were given some bread after boarding, but it was also frozen to the extent that it was completely impervious to the attack of the strongest teeth. We tried to thaw out our bread rations by all possible means, by putting them under our arms, on the stomachs, even between the legs.

At long last we heard the noise of the diesel engines, the sound of the ship's horn and the motor vessel was on its way. Rough weather set in soon after departure, but nobody lay down, as it would have meant certain death from freezing. Instead, we sat on our bunks like sparrows on a perch and looked at the floor. A real ball was taking place on the floor of the hold! It was lit with electric lights and freezing men were jumping on its floor and were performing a macabre dance. Pairs of these unfortunates were dancing, falling, jumping up and continuing their tragic dance. A magnificent ball indeed! I thought that I heard a happy music, the sound of Satan's own band.

Suddenly, some poorly constructed wooden bunks situated across the aisle from us gave way and collapsed on the floor of the hold with a deafening sound accompanied by blood-curdling animal-like screams of their occupants. The wrecked structures were pulled apart and lying on the iron floor under them we saw a horrifying picture of squashed pancake-like forms, an agglomeration of ghastly figurines, looking like dolls made out of dough. They were taken to the deck and, as we were later told, thrown overboard....

The December days of 1947 were an utter horror, which live in my memory as a turbid nightmare. Our frozen through transport ship "Krasnogvardeets" was battling the elements on its way from Vanino Bay to Nakhodka and the noise of its diesel engines was accompanied by the screams of its passengers. Fights broke out for a place on a bunk, a bowl of thin broth or an effort to retain the smallest amount of warmth in one's frail body. The hunger and cold were unimaginable...

Whose unhesitating hand sent us all to our death?

First and foremost it belonged to Stalin. His thesis about the "inevitable sharpening of the class warfare" unleashed dark forces in the land and opened the road towards the settlement of personal scores, towards an unfettered control over people's destinies, by criminals. Naturally enough, the right of that arbitrary rule was given to senior Communist Party officials. Nothing could be done without phone calls and written instructions (signed in an unintelligible scrawl) from those people. The well-fed rosy-cheeked perfumed potbellied generals and colonels of the NKVD-MGB (*former name of the KGB MH*) had, as a rule, never taken part in any military action. They used nepotism and various other connections to establish themselves in the warm offices of the GULAG and USVITL(*Russian acronym for "The Control Centre for the North-Eastern Prison Camps" MH*). These drones used to smoke Stalin's favourite "Herzegovina Flor" and "Belomorcanal" cigarettes with cardboard mouth pieces (*"papirosy" in Russian MH*) and drink imported coffee laced with Armenian cognac. They used to exchange obscene stories and to paw their giggling female secretaries...They used to push around their subordinates and issue orders of the kind: "Load into the holds of the vacant 'Liberty' motor vessel so many people—correction— not people—prisoners; send them to such and such a destination..."

Clearly, if the transportation had involved cattle or sheep, for which Moscow would have held them responsible, these inhuman creatures would have taken care with the way the job was done. What would be the repercussions if the animals froze to death in temperatures of under thirty degrees? However, here they were "only" dealing with four thousand "enemies of the people"—an abundant species, found in all corners of their vast Motherland. What is there to worry about? Just lift the receiver and issue an order: "send so many from hither to thither" – and the task is accomplished!

It took our vessel three days to reach the port of Nakhodka, but the ship and its freezing passengers were kept waiting for another day, by which time all warmth generated by its engines had dissipated. When we docked at last and the prisoners were ordered to disembark, more than half of us were unable to move. Several hundred corpses were taken off the ship to be disposed of on the top of a hill, and the rest of us semi-invalid "passengers" left the pier walking as a disorganised rabble.

I had a badly frostbitten great toe, but was still able to stagger out of the ship on my own and the stinking prison hut reminded me of paradise. I managed to exchange my bread rations for a very decent knee length sheepskin coat. That was a fair exchange, as a warm coat was worth the absence of a day's ration of bread. However, my joy was premature, as I lost my coat given to me in Vanino to some disgusting thief during a nightly visit to the toilet, which meant that I had to wear the coat on my naked body. In the meantime, my frostbitten toe got infected and was blue and swollen. Luckily, I was taken to the hospital where I refused to have it amputated and was given proper medical help.

I'll never forget Dr. Belyavsky, a fellow-prisoner, a skinny, stooping man who had been imprisoned since 1937, having been to Kolyma and heaven knows where else, but retained his humanity. He took pity on me and kept me in the hospital for a few extra days as an orderly, although lifers were not allowed to hold those positions, and he was taking a great risk in giving me a chance to properly recover.

The small hospital in a hut in the port of Nakhodka was the best holiday resort I had ever stayed in my life. It was warm, I was given hospital rations, medical treatment and had access to a trough, which allowed me to have a wash, and I was given 200 grams of white bread for breakfast!

I stayed in a room with two tiers of bunks—three men below—three above. Many of them were returning from Chukotka because they were too ill to work in the Gulag. Most of their fellow prisoners died after two years hard labour in the ice fields of the Schmidt Promontory on the shores of the Arctic Ocean. My companions survived but had become invalids. Their Documents were being processed by the authorities and every day some of them received train tickets and dry rations for a trip home, consisting of bread, herring and sugar. Some were heading for Siberia, others for the Ukraine, Russia or Byelorussia. My two companions were Ivan and Lyoshka. Ivan kept talking about his relatives, saying with a shy smile: "I won't be able to do a proper day's work, but should be able to work as a watchman in a collective farm, but at least I'll be able to see my parents and my homeland. It is all the fault of my damned imprisonment by the Germans after they surrounded my company..." All of them were being punished for having been POWs. Lyoshka did not say much, but was always hungry and made no reference to his family.

One morning Ivan was called in to see the paramedic to have his injection ordered by the doctor. We could clearly see Ivan through the worn sheet, which served as a curtain. His arm was bent and the paramedic was giving him the needle. The curtain parted a short while later and Ivan walked slowly to his seat, with one finger pressing on the cotton wool covering the injection spot. An orderly was distributing our morning rations of a piece of white bread each. My piece was placed on my table and Ivan and Lyoshka had theirs placed on a small table to the right of the passageway between the bunks. Ivan smiled when he saw the bread and moved towards it bypassing a stretcher bed, which was in his way, when suddenly he exclaimed "Ow—ow!", lost his balance, sat on the stretcher bed, then lied down, uttered a long wailing sound and lay still...

The patients started shouting, Dr. Belyakovsky ran in, felt Ivan's pulse gave him an injection of camphor, but it was too late.. The long-suffering Ivan was dead.

At that moment I heard a strange grunting sound and saw the silent Lyoshka choking whilst shoving the dry piece of Ivan's bread into his mouth and pushing his piece under the pillow...

Chapter 4: Nakhodka

Unfortunately it was not long before I had to leave the warm pleasant hospital and was sent to a normal hut, which had to accommodate extra prisoners. There was no place for them not only on the bunks but also on the floor. I walked past sitting and walking men and found a seat after unceremoniously shoving aside two emaciated inmates, although it was impossible to lie down. Despite the fact that I had already been through the mill, I was terrified at what I saw. The stuffy dark hut was poorly lit and was full of a heap of bodies. The mere act of trying to rest one's arm, leg or lying down required a huge effort. The mass of bodies reminded me of a cesspit with worms crawling on its surface... The resemblance was so strong that I felt as if I myself were a worm. The whole mob was snoring, squelching, moaning and uttering heavy breathing sounds.

The other end of the hut presented an entirely different picture of a happy crowd of well-dressed young and old professional criminals who were sitting on a separate bunk and merrily playing a guitar. They were laughing, telling jokes, playing cards and generally raising merry hell.

If one of that crowd had to go to the toilet or just outside, he would never try to do so carefully or to find a passage between the other prisoners. Oh no, the culprit would jump on the human mass from the bunk and trample on people's heads, shoulders, legs or other body parts with his heavy boots with iron heels on his way out, to the accompaniment of the guitar and a happy laughter of his comrades. All one could hear were the cries of pain from the political prisoners, which gave the impression that the callous crim was playing a human piano using his victims as live keys....

Once every ten days we were marched to a bathhouse where our clothes were subjected to a mandatory heat treatment to eradicate body lice. Our warm undershirts, pants and underwear were attached to a ring bearing an identification number and forwarded to the heat chamber, with an identical number hung on the prisoner's neck. One assistant bathhouse manager used to plonk a small quantity of liquid soap on the prisoner's head, with the second attendant handing him a tub of warm water. That was all we were entitled to, with some lucky devils managing to double up on these rations. The washing time was very short and we had to quickly find our way to the exit where we were given our clothes. The clothes were being returned by the professional criminals who threw the bundles of clothes with their attached identification numbers on the floor. Needless to say, the stinking clothes were deformed by the heat and the skeleton-like prisoners had to identify them shouting: "This is my bundle! Give it to me!" Some bundles were handed over, others were thrown.

I remember saying politely after the first visit to the bathhouse: "That one is mine! Hand it to me please!" My God, what a "comedy"! The crims were ecstatic: "Did you hear that? A rotten intellectual! Please! Here you are, scum!"– and my bundle was kicked in my direction like a soccer ball. I did not say anything, but when my number was called out after the second visit to the bathhouse, screamed in a rough voice: "That's mine, you bastard—give it to me!"

The clothes were immediately handed to me with some indication that I induced a certain amount of fear in the crims. That's how one learns to survive in that environment, with death awaiting the meek...

I was unable to understand why I encountered so many people upon my return from the hospital. I noticed a few groups of young people who seemed to look very much alike. I found myself next to a few of them and found out that they were former POWs who returned to Russia of their own free will. They told me that after their release in Germany they were taken to France and then to the USA. They told me that their stay in the US was quite pleasant. They were given good clothes and food and were offered work. Life was getting organised, but all that was interrupted by visits from the Russian Embassy staff who urged them to return home. Everybody had been pardoned, they said, and nobody was guilty anyway. Any rumours of arrests and deportations to Siberia were dastardly enemy propaganda and their relatives and friends were waiting for them. Anybody wishing to return to Russia would be repatriated at government expense on specially chartered ships, which would take them from Seattle to Nakhodka where they would be met with an orchestra

Some of the POWs did not believe the promises and stayed behind, but this lot did and were loaded on quite comfortable vessels for the trip home. The comfort lasted only during the sea voyage and in Nakhodka they were met by a military escort and most of them finished up getting 25 years in the Gulag, to be served in the North, where they joined many other former soldiers. I remember one of them—an Uzbek by the name of Islam Aliyev. He and I spent nearly two years working in the same place.

"In 1941 my unit was surrounded by the Germans and our platoon commander gave an order to surrender, which we did and spent the rest of the war working in Germany. We were repatriated at war's end and again found ourselves in prison. The investigator asked me: 'Why did you surrender instead of shooting yourself?' ' I wanted to live.' 'OK–then, you will live in the Far North for the next ten years.'"

Aliyev was one of the lucky ones who came home, but countless others like him found their graves in the permafrost of the Arctic.

It was not long before I, being an escapee, was sent to ZUR (Russian for the "Zone of Special Security"). It was very cold and prisoners did not stay outside for longer than they had to, but a pale prisoner, an acquaintance of mine, called Petka, asked me to stay...

"Do you want to earn an extra ration of bread?"

"Of course! What do I have to do?"

"Come with me and I'll show you."

I followed him to a wooden timber outhouse which stood at the end of the yard where Petka stood near a crow bar which was covered in frozen excreta, fished out a 500 gram piece of bread from underneath his shirt, put his foot on a protruding timber plank and said:

"Hit it with the bar—the bread is yours if you break my leg. I am at the end of my tether. Let them declare me an invalid. "

Petka gave me a pitiful pleading look of a hunted animal, but I whispered:

"Sorry, mate, I can't do it. Find somebody else".

He must have found somebody else because I had not seen him since...

The spring was slow in coming, but it was followed by a particularly lovely summer of 1948. All of us were waiting for transportation to the North, which dominated all our conversations. Columns of Japanese soldiers, survivors of the Japanese Kwantung Army were marched past our camp on their way home, which they were to undertake by sea, but the life in the ZUR had not changed. We spent most daylight hours lying about in the sun on our worn bedding and indulging in talk about life outside prison and general trivial matters.

ZUR bordered on a women's camp and our crims quickly established a friendship with the young female thieves. Despite the fact that the political prisoners were starving, our crooks were not only well fed but also given such luxuries as white bread and small carcasses of salted red fish. They shouted over the fence: "Manka, wait for me! I am coming over soon!" and threw their luxurious rations over the barbed wire, while we, hungry political prisoners, were lying down away from that merriment. I noted with some irony that faced with the choice of being offered one of the buxom wenches or a loaf of white bread and some red fish, I, despite my then 37 years, would have undoubtedly chosen the latter... Everything is relative in this world...

A few days later I became a witness to an inner political struggle inside our hut, where there were three tiers of bunks made of timber of timber poles. I was having an afternoon nap on a top bunk when I heard a shouted command: "Everybody out into the yard! Hurry! On the double!" It took me a while to wake up and it was too late for me to obey it, as some stragglers were already fleeing the building trying to protect their heads with their hands from the savage blows of the sticks wielded by the senior criminals and their sidekicks. I stayed in my place, lying flat on my stomach so as not to be noticed and saw the goings on in the hut through the gaps between the poles.

The criminal fraternity of those days consisted of the so-called "honest thieves" and "bitches." Whereas the former did not do any work in the camp themselves, the latter became active collaborators of the prison administration, organising the beating of political prisoners with sticks, maintaining prison discipline and making sure that those unfortunates worked hard and obeyed the instructions of the guards. As mentioned, the "honest thieves" did not follow those precepts, which resulted in a blood feud between the two groups.

The "bitches" ran the roost in Nakhodka in the summer of 1948, a situation, which was supported by the camp administration, which overlooked the brutal methods used by their favourites. The episode I witnessed was one of the facets of the power struggle mentioned above.

The "honest ones" were being brought in one by one and asked: "Well? Are you going to join us? If so, kiss!" I stayed motionless so as not to be discovered, and therefore was unable to see what it was that the victims had to kiss—it could have been a knife or the undone fly of the senior "bitch." Those who changed their allegiance and kissed whatever it was, were let go, whereas any dissidents were picked up and thrown onto the floor so that they fell on their backs. One heard a heavy muted thud and a scream: "What are you doing, Brothers?!", but it made no impression on the thugs who kept repeating the performance, shouting: "Come on, boys! One—two—three!" The lifeless bodies of the recalcitrants were thrown into a corner and it was clear that they would not survive due to internal injuries.

The "honest ones" got their revenge later, after Stalin's death in 1953, when I was already a so-called "free worker." I remember the arrival of a large prison train and the surviving "bitches" running screamingly to the guard house begging for their lives, and the authorities sending them away out of harm's way, as a reward for past services.

Another feature of life in the ZUR was the hunt for gold teeth. The crims went hunting in packs of six, looking into the mouths of the inmates and extracting any golden crowns. It was possible to occasionally escape these thugs in the general camp, but ZUR comprising a single hut, there was nowhere to hide. The thugs used to work at night. They would corner the unfortunate victim, choke or stun him and let him go only after the crowns, together with his teeth, would be in their hands. It was heart-rending to see a grown strong man who had been a proud owner of a few gold crowns, sporting a black toothless cavity of a mouth and crying in utter despair at his loss.

My mouth had been well looked after by my late former mother-in-law Yelena Pavlovna Maslakova, who was a popular dentist in the town of Harbin. She fitted me with a crown and a couple of bridges made of high quality gold and I never remembered her effort until the damned ZUR, when I smiled whilst having a conversation with a criminal by the name of Pashka Starinsky, who immediately said:

"Listen, let me have your crown! I desperately need it! I am going to give you a piece of bread and a sliver of butter for it now and will continue to supply you with rations!

I realised that the alternative to this offer meant that I would lose all the gold in my mouth, plus all my teeth, one fine night, and decided to part with one crown. Pashka pulled it out and gave me the promised food. However, he immediately forgot about his other promise, and I knew from personal experience that one was not supposed to remind the thugs of such things. Unfortunately, I still had the bridges in my mouth and realised that they too were sought after.

What was I to do? I had some mates in our hut, people with whom I shared my meals. I resolved to sell my teeth when I saw a middle-aged man crying in utter desperation at the loss of his crowns, of which he was very proud only one day ago, and displaying his hideous empty mouth, which did not contain one single tooth! There was nobody he could complain to or who could offer any protection. We were at the mercy of a pack of wolves and were their victims because we had no weapons.

I made a pact with the senior cook. In return for my golden bridges he agreed to scoop the daily rations of soup given to me and my mates from the bottom of the cooking pot, which made them more nutritious...

However, it was easier said than done, as the removal of the bridges had to be carried out away from the prying eyes. We found old bits of iron which we used as dental tools, hid in a dark corner on the third level of the bunks, which was stuffy and was so close to the ceiling that one could only sit in a contorted position, and started the complicated operation in the feeble light from a distant window. I was kneeling and supporting my jaws to prevent them from being broken by the tool. My mates were trying to wrench the bridges from my teeth by lifting the metal and hitting the tool with a makeshift hammer. Occasionally I found the pain unbearable and uttered muted moans whilst spitting blood. However, strange though it may seem, I felt a sense of immense relief when the bridges were finally removed, as I still had my own, albeit filed down, teeth and there was no more danger of having them knocked out.

We had the additional "joy", which lasted for a fortnight, of a daily serving of thick soup full of sharp fish bones, which were mercilessly hurting my bare gums.

Chapter 5: North Of The Arctic Circle

Most of us, a grey mass of humanity were resigned to the transportation to the North, but instances of self-mutilation became more frequent the closer it came to that day. The cutting off or braking of legs or arms belonged to extreme measures punishable by law, which resulted in an increase of a sentence. However, there existed more sophisticated methods, such as punching a hole in the skin of a limb and infecting the wound by inserting into it a piece of string covered in the from dirty teeth. That string was later removed to eliminate the evidence. The result was a major infection, sometimes requiring an operation.

Another method involved crushing the sugar rations into a fine powder and inhaling it for several days. That produced a bloody cough. And yet another way was to get some manganese chloride disinfectant from the first aid room and to sprinkle it into the eyes, which often resulted in blindness. I was aghast at the sight of these shenanigans and thought to myself: "Oh God, men throughout the ages worked, robbed and even killed for the sake of getting a cure, and here I see these unfortunates ready to pay to lose their health!"

A corpulent Ukrainian by the name of Alexander Oleinik walked up to me one day feeling his way around the yard and started talking to me in muffled sepulchral voice. He had rosy cheeks and his eyes, which were covered with downcast lids, like those of a fairy-tale ghost, had long feminine eyelashes. He was blind having used too much manganese chloride in the hope of being invalidated and allowed to avoid the transportation to the dreaded North, but he was being transported with everybody else. He asked me to bring him food and to the toilet. Alexander was a quiet pleasant handsome clever and, it seemed, God-fearing fellow. For two months I would bring him food and lead him by the hand around the camp...Some sceptical prisoners laughed at me saying: ". Sashka (*short for Alexander MH)* realises that you are an easy touch and is telling you lies. He can see perfectly well, but is putting on an act..."

However, I kept stubbornly looking after that unfortunate right up to the 16th of July when we were loaded into the four dark holds of the ship "Stepan Razin", which were equipped with sleeping bunks. There was very little room but Sashka and I managed to squeeze ourselves onto the lower bunk where we sat down. It took me a while to get used to the darkness but I was nearly speechless when I was finally able to see Sashka's face, as he was quietly staring at me with his huge wide open eyes.

CHAPTER 5

"How could you be so deceitful, Sashka!?"—exclaimed I.

"Well, Yuryevich *("son of George", s in Russian MH)*, we all have to try to save our skins in our own way. I believed right to the end that they would not send a blind man to Kolyma, but I was wrong. Don't worry, I'll never forget your kindness. Who knows, we might be able to stage an escape together one day!"

In the event, we did not manage to escape, but we did travel together to Pevek, where our roads parted. We did meet again six years later in the mine called Yuzhny *("Southern" in Russian MH)*0 by which time we had both been freed and Sashka was getting ready to leave Chukotka. He was released in Pevek, managed to buy and raise a few pigs and to sell their meat at exorbitant prices prevailing in Chukotka at the time, which made him a well-to-do man. Sashka showed me two savings bank books, which contained seventy five thousand of the "old" currency (there had been a money reform later). He remembered my help and asked me if he could help me in any way, but I did not need any assistance by that time.

Getting back to that hot day in Nakhodka, our ship with a red band painted on its chimney together with the name "Libertos" sounded a farewell siren and left the pier of the port of Nakhodka, a port, which had seen innumerable human tragedies.

Our first stop was Port Vanino where we picked up some provisions and then continued north through the Tatar Straits. We circumnavigated the southern end of the Sakhalin Island, sailed through the Laperouse Straits and entered the Sea of Okhotsk. It was hot and crowded in the holds. Fresh bead had run out and our daily rations consisted of 200 grams of rusks and two servings of soup. Water which was lowered into the hold in a large wooden barrel was the source of constant fights. Most prisoners were suffering from terrible thirst, whereas the hardened criminals poured into pots and even managed to wash. We all sat on the bunks and were sweating profusely.

Toilet breaks involved climbing a long vertical ladder and sitting on a makeshift toilet seat hanging over the water. One evening I was deliberately taking my time in that contraption. Our motor vessel was speeding east with its motors making a low level sound. We were going around the Island of Sakhalin. The purple-grey sea was absolutely calm, and on the starboard side I could see small fishing vessels with their yellow lights and the outline of a hilly shore, most likely that of the Japanese Island of Hokkaido. "What if I jump off now?'—thought I— "they may not notice my escape." That was my last chance, because Chukotka meant the end! Since receiving a sentence of 25 years I never stopped thinking of an escape. My thoughts were interrupted by a sharp shout, which sounded like a gun shot in the calm air:

"Stop mucking about! Get down and into the hold at once!"

I woke up from my daydream and saw a security guard hiding behind a chimney of the ship. There is no doubt that he would have riddled me with bullets had I jumped into the water.

The mountains of the port of Vanino were covered in pink blossoms of the willow herb and I thought that I saw that scene for the last time. However, the last similar picture was of the pinkish and pale-green shores of the Providenye (*Russian for Providence MH*) Bay in the Bering Sea, after which all we saw was ice. It got very cold and the prisoners put on any and all clothes they had with them. Large ice floes were frequently hitting the sides of the ship. During my rare visits to the deck, I saw that we were sailing through the Bering Straits in the wake of the powerful icebreaker "Ilya Muromets", which carved a blue-white corridor through the ice. The bare rocky shores of Chukotka were on our port side and distant Alaska could be seen through the mist to the starboard.

We started hearing rumours that there were some seamen and radio operators on board our ship who were going to stage a mutiny, arrest the guards and take us to the American shore. We also heard that crowbars and boat-hooks had been hidden in the holds and that everybody had to be ready for a signal...It seems, though, that the mutineers were betrayed. There followed a mass search for weapons and the organisers of the mutiny were thrown into the isolation cell.

In the meantime, the hungry, cold and wild life of the holds went on. The criminals were stealing the last rusks and rags from the political prisoners, bashed the recalcitrants senseless, gambled away the proceeds of their robberies, and sometimes gambled away even their own lives.

A few losers who refused to pay up were publicly executed. The executioners would wrap the neck of a condemned man in a towel and pull on each end whilst supporting their feet on his shoulders. The victim barely had time to whisper : "Brootheers!.." He turned blue, his tongue fell out of his mouth, and very soon his body was floating in the water, which was splashing underneath the lowest bunk.

In the meantime, our motor vessel kept forging ahead, with its diesel engines making rumbling sounds and was beginning to turn in the north-westerly direction, first into the Chukotsk- and later the East-Siberian Sea. Having left Nakhodka on the 16th pf August of 1948 we arrived in Pevek on the 29th of August, having covered seven thousand nautical miles and spent 44 days below decks.

Chapter 6: Chukotka

The township of Pevek greeted us with its white silent cover. It was snowing lightly and we saw the pier, and on the shore were small houses, some three-, four- and two-storied buildings, and clay huts. There were snow-covered low hills behind the township and snow, snow everywhere. Our "Stepan Razin" docked at a low jetty.

The gangway was lowered, we walked down its shaky boards and marched to the edge of the township where we entered an empty prison camp surrounded by barbed wire. We started shovelling snow and putting up large canvas tents, in which stood several empty oil barrels. They were the customary stoves used everywhere North of the Arctic Circle, and their fuel consisted of saw dust mixed with used lubricating oil. Normal camp news started flooding each tent, such as that the toilet vessels were going to be delivered soon, or that the most terrifying mine was known as "The Valley of Death", from which nobody came back alive...

It so happened that already on the third day of our arrival we were taken to that mine in a customary open lorry, which was chock-a-block full of squatting prisoners who were crammed like herrings in a barrel. The seemingly infinitely long road through the tundra led past bare rocky snow-covered hills. A nagging thought pursued me:"Yes, this is definitely my last trip. I doubt whether I'll ever leave this place alive."

Having reached a settlement on the 47th kilometre of the road, we saw a flock of grey wild geese with clipped wings rushing away from the truck. We were told that there were thousands of these birds migrating to Chukotka in summer and that the locals caught them and ate them in autumn. It would be nice to catch one of them and to devour it alive! I was not sure what the camp rations were like. Was it 600, 700 or 800 grams of bread? It was a constantly burning question for all inmates: will I ever have enough black bread to eat before I die? We did not think of meat or any other delicacies. All our thoughts were about bread and thick wheat porridge. Nothing else seemed to exist.

Finally we arrived at our destination, the so-called "Separate Camp Site" (OLP in Russian MH). It consisted of a rectangular block of land located on a slight incline of a white completely bare hill, near a stony river and surrounded by several rows of barbed wire. Four watchtowers were guarding its perimeter and a nearby white administrative building was the home for the guards. Further on were long low prison huts situated on a hillock. There were also a dining room and a store-room. So-called "toilets" were located at the side of the camp, distinguished by the sight of stalactites consisting of human excreta. A row of white pyramids, which stood outside the camp, turned out to be mounds of ore obtained from the mine.

We finally reached the dining room. The portion of bread given to us before we left Pevek was a distant memory by that time, but here we were served a hot soup made of fish heads garnished with some sort of a cereal. The main thing was that the cook was not yet familiar with people's faces and it was possible to walk up to the kitchen window twice or even three times and receive additional servings of the soup. The only precaution used was to change the way one's hat was sitting on the head... The next step was to lie down on the bunk and to become divorced from reality. Vague thoughts came to mind in those moments: "Well, maybe things will work out after all?" I was only 37 and did not want to think of near and unavoidable death.

I don't remember whether we were given a day off, but the first days of our truly hard labour were unforgettable. At 6am sharp ("can it be the end of the night's rest?"—I thought) the lamp outside our hut was turned off and a sound of a rail being hit with a hammer— which felt like a blow to the back of the head—signalled the reveille. I raced to the toilet, then to the dining room, where the breakfast consisted of a scoop of soup, half a piece of bread, some weak slightly sweet tea -and off!

We stood in rows behind the prison gate and were led out in formations of five. "First, second...tenth" counted the guard. Then followed the order: "Walk in formation! A step to the left, a step to the right—I'll shoot without warning! Go!"

The work site, which was to be surrounded by armed soldiers, was within two kilometres of the camp. Our tools lying in a heap near a smithy consisted of crowbars, shovels and picks. Fights broke out over the tools because stronger implements made it easier to achieve the cursed standard output. From the smithy to the worksite the prisoners walked on their own, since the guards were dispatched to surround its perimeter. I was walking at the rear of that strange detachment and it seemed to me that I was following a medieval army, with crowbars and shovels carried on the shoulders of the identical dark stooped figures looking like ancient lances and halberds in the eerie light of the waning moon. The snow was crunching under the feet of the unfortunates who looked like monsters out of a children's fairy- tale.

The ore was mined on the hillside using an open-cut method. Every prisoner had a pick, a shovel and a wheelbarrow, which had to be filled with the ore and wheeled 100 to 150 metres over shaky narrow gangways, where it was emptied and taken back to the pit-face along parallel gangways. The standard output per 12-hour shift, which included the march to and from the mine and the time spent on lunch, was 40 barrows. Standard food rations for the first three days were 600 grams of bread per day, with up to 900 grams in subsequent days, depending upon the level of one's output. Anybody who failed to achieve the standard output after 3 days was punished with the reduction of rations to 30 grams, which meant that these prisoners were condemned to death, as a hungry man had no chance of delivering 40 barrows a day.

Work was generally carried out in pairs, with one man breaking up the surface and the other one shovelling it into the wheelbarrow. The wheelbarrows were pushed in tandem, so as to help a mate lift his cart on to the gangway if it fell off. However, on occasions, I used to fall off the gangplank together with the ore, which was instantly followed by an impatient: "Get out of the way!"- from the next man.

I shall never forget the facial expression and the voice of my workmate, polite well-educated native of Kiev, Fedya Simonenko, a senior lieutenant, who was sentenced to hard labour for having been captured in an unconscious state by the Germans.

...One evening we were loading the last wheelbarrows. Our arms and legs were shaking, we were at the end of our tether, but there was still no siren signalling the end of the shift. We looked at each other like trapped animals and Fedya muttered, his face grey and lifeless:

"You know, I spent a lot of time on the front, but I never felt that death was so near, right next to me..."

A professional criminal—the worst type of human scum– who was working as an assistant foreman, started cursing us on top of his voice:

"Why have you stopped, you bastards?! Get on with it! Move! And if you don't, I'll show you what easy life is really like!"

A guard stationed at the end of our section started shouting something, but we stood there unable to shift the cursed wheelbarrow, when the sound of the siren located at the bottom of the hill shattered the intolerable silence. End of shift! Thank God! We can drop the wheelbarrow and head for "home"—to wit the prison camp!

A swarthy peasant by the name of Kopylov was the champion worker who used to be able to deliver 45 barrows per shift. He was praised as a model for other workers, a newssheet with his name was put on the wall of our hut and he was rewarded with 900 grams of bread and a cube of slimy porridge in gelatine. Kopylov felt like a hero, eating his rations on a top bunk, but his triumph did not last long: he got a hernia, fell ill and was soon dead.

Fedya and I set no records and were content with our 700 grams. Strangely enough, we gradually got used to our workload and felt that we could survive. Unfortunately, I was quite unexpectedly sent to a hard labour prison, because my papers contained a red line, indicating that I belonged to a group of prisoners who had escaped or attempted an escape.

The hard labour prison stood in the centre of a valley fairly far away from the camp and was surrounded with its own fence complete with watchtowers. It was divided into two halves: the first one contained criminals and the other—political detainees. Our previous labour camp was a real paradise compared with that prison.

Our half of the prison received practically no heating. After returning from work we used to be lined up on its cement floor and were ordered to strip bare, after which we were most exhaustively searched to ensure that we had no hidden implements, such as a razor blade, a nail or a piece of wire, which could have been used to pick a lock. "Run!"—was the command issued after the search, whereupon we picked up the heap of our belongings, clothes and shoes and ran to our cells, which had wooden floors and commenced to dance and jump wildly in order to warm up. Strangely enough, very few prisoners got sick.

The quarry where we worked in autumn was closed in winter due to extreme cold, and we were then required to work on the preparation of mine shafts. That's how it was done.

Four red flags were placed in the corners of a snow-covered white field and two guards armed with rifles stood on its sides. Pegs were placed inside the larger square, which divided it into something resembling a chessboard. Each of them indicated the positions of a future mine shaft and was allocated to one prisoner. The prisoner had to clear the snow and to gouge out a vertical hole in the frozen soil using an ice-cold crow bar and often wearing torn mittens. The holes had a cylindrical shape, 45 centimetres in diameter, and the worker removed the crushed frozen soil with a tin "spoon' attached to a wooden handle. The morning standard was four 45 centimetre holes per prisoner, after which the crew was taken to a dug-out to get some warmth and the job was taken over by the explosives experts who loaded ammonium nitrate into the holes, attached fuses to the explosives and blasted the soil. We had to grab our shovels and throw the loosened soil to the surface. This produced a 1.2 long by 0.8 metre wide beginning of a shaft, whose depth had to reach between 3 and 4 metres. By that time the shaft extended deeper than a layer of turf and reached the tin-bearing ore called "cassiterite".

It took me about ten days to reach the depth of 3.5 metres of my first shaft. The deeper I dug, the warmer it got, but the harder it was to throw the soil to the surface, as half of it fell back over my head and into the eyes. Blasting chambers were dug in completed shafts. They were filled with explosives, which were detonated, thus enabling the bulldozers to remove all the soil covering the surface of the mine. The exposed ore was then mined and sent to a washing plant.

We spent two months in the hard labour prison during which time we lost two mates. The first one was a young silly fellow everybody called "Lodochka" (*"A small boat"*, *in Russian MH)*. He was constantly singing songs of the underworld, one of which featured a little boat—hence his nickname. The "bitches" liked his singing and gave him extra food. In order to thank his benefactors Lodochka shouted one morning when all prisoners were assembled in rows before marching to work:

"Truman, come here! Help us!"

Harry Truman was the American president at the time. The crims liked the joke and laughed heartily. The guards looked at each other, called for silence and marched us to work. I picked up my crow bar and suddenly felt a dreadful sadness. To hell with this trench and everything else! Why should I work as a slave? Will there ever be an end to my suffering? I have no more energy left! I sat down in the corner of the trench and closed my eyes, but soon realised that I was about to freeze to death. That made me make a resolution: "Keep at it while you can. Nobody is going to carry your burden for you.." That philosophical formula has since helped me many times. I picked up the crow bar and started to break up the soil, when a shot sounded all of a sudden on the surface of the mine. We all stopped work and scrambled aloft.

"Lodochka' was lying on the edge of the white field, almost on the border delineated by an imaginary line leading from one red flag to the next. A red line led from his temple to the surface of the snow. Somebody tried to go near him, but the guard nearest to the dead man barked:

"Don't go near him! Back to work!"

A car arrived soon from the camp and took our mate away. He was gone forever... We all understood that he paid the ultimate price for calling out Truman's name. The experienced prisoners among us were sure that Lodochka was trapped by a guard, standing behind the forbidden line and calling him over offering him a smoke. The simple lad crossed that line and was shot dead at a short range. Why else would Lodochka cross into the forbidden zone?

"The bitches" and "honest thieves" had a good time in our cell. In the evenings they composed stories of the type: "A black limousine with its headlights turned off was racing along the streets of London or Paris...", sang songs or played cards, which they artistically produced from unknown materials. The inhabitants of lower banks were not privy to the wagers used in card games or to what games were actually played. Those matters were reserved for the aristocracy inhabiting the upper bunks. I was occasionally invited to join the elite and to tell them stories about the life abroad, for which I was rewarded with makhorka. "Come on, tell us about women and tigers"—they would demand. Very popular were stories about tiger hunts and about Japanese bathhouses where naked wives visited their husbands in the men's section of those establishments. Other favourites were tales about Shanghai dance halls and cabarets, in which clients were served drinks at tables located under palm trees placed along the walls, and the paid female dance partners came from all countries of Europe and Asia.

Most professional criminals had hyphenated nicknames, such as Kolka-Chelita, Vaska-Kandyba, Vitka-Meteorite, Kolka-Cherkess etc. Amongst them was a powerful, quick, talkative and humorous lad from Kazakhstan with the nickname of Sashka-Zveryok *("Zveryok" means "small animal" in Russian MH)*. Unfortunately, he lost in a gambling contest, i.e. he placed a bet, without being able to cover it, and lost, which in accordance with the laws of the criminal fraternity meant that he had to be executed, and the court of the criminal elders appointed Kolka-Chilita to be the executioner. None of the uninitiated, to wit political prisoners, knew or were allowed to know anything about it.

One day I was hard at work at the bottom of a three metre deep mineshaft breaking up a tough granite rock when I noticed Kolka-Chilita sitting on his haunches and peering into the opening.

"What do you want?"

"Ah, it is you!"–giggled Kolka –"But I thought..."

I had no idea what he was thinking, but soon heard a muffled cry from a nearby shaft:

"What are you doing?!" –followed by a short scuffle and the sound of whistles from the guards. I crawled out of my shaft and immediately understood what had taken place. Zveryok's shaft was next to mine, and Chelita was stalking the wrong man at first. However, having found his quarry, he immediately sunk a pick into his skull.

Chelita was serving the maximum allowable sentence of 25 years, and could therefore serve no more time. As far as I can recall, the authorities did not even bother to try him.

We were returned to the ordinary camp after that incident, and I thought that I was almost back home. On my arrival at the camp I met a few of my countrymen from Manchuria, who were a source of support and great comfort for me; two of them my old acquaintances. The first one was a native of Harbin by the name of Boris Pavlovich Kadochnikov whom I met at the Handaokhedsey station located on the eastern branch of the Eastern Chinese Railway, and the other—Pyotr Kalugin—a hunter and Old Believer *(a member of a break away Russian Orthodox Church MH)*, who lived in a village called Romanovka, which is also located on the eastern branch of that Railway.

A well-educated Boris Pavlovich worked as an assistant to our camp doctor, who was also a prisoner. He used to keep a list of sick inmates and was able to give an inmate a day off from slave labour. I decided to ask him for that favour on the eve of my birthday. I went to see him after work and joined a throng of prisoners who were also trying to get some sick leave. I was healthy and had no fever. However, even though I knew how to raise the reading of a thermometer by giving it a few taps, I did not want to get Boris into trouble, because the criminal working in the hospital would easily discover my ruse, which could have cost him his job. I was at a loss as to what to do, and decided to say a few words to him in an Asian language. Most Russian émigrés had some Japanese, but I was not sure about Boris, and decided to mutter in

Chinese that I was turning 38 the following day. He understood my request, gave me a day off, and I have never forgotten that favour.

I first met Pyotr Kalugin, a huge man with a dark beard of the type one sees on old icons, at a remote railway station in the north-east of Manchuria. He was surrounded by his light-brown or red-bearded fellow Old Believers and stood near home-made cages containing two recently captured tiger cubs who were hissing, snarling and bearing their white fangs. My brother Arseny and I were sending the tigers to Harbin together with a few dozen frozen carcasses of wild pigs and goats, which we shot in the nearby hills. They were frozen stiff and resembled lumps of wood. We all stood on the railway platform and the colourful group of bearded lads was surrounded by its dogs. Having introduced ourselves, we started waiting for a train, whose whistle stop lasted only for two or three minutes, but that gave our crowd enough time to throw through the open doors of the railway carriage the tiger cages and the frozen game.

Thus started the friendship of two families of professional hunters, which continued in the Old Believers' village of Romanovka and continued in Chukotka. However, I barely recognised Kalugin in Chukotka because he had shaven off his beard, although his deep voice, sounding as if it was coming from a barrel, remained the same. He grew his beard again after his release from the Gulag, but by that time it had quite a few grey hair...

A fellow-Manchurian by the name of Pyotr Xenofontovich Kvasov, whom I had not known before, became my closest friend in the Far

North who before his arrest used to be an engine driver on the Western Section of the Chinese Eastern Railway. He was a thick set swarthy man, which is common in people with an admixture of Buryat blood, and was a highly principled individual. He had a moustache, which was a rarity amongst the prisoners of the Gulag.

He worked as an engine driver at the Power Station of my "Special Purposes Camp Number 3", was not supervised by prison guards and was friendly with truck drivers, who were not prisoners. That enabled him to get bread and brick-tea. When I arrived in the camp, he welcomed me with some bread and real tea, which had nothing in common with the yellowish dishwater, our cooks passed for tea in the camp. He read and heard about our family in a magazine called "Rubezh" *("Boundary", in Russian MH),*which used to be published in Harbin and we used to meet and talk after work.

I would sip his magnificent tea and Pyotr would philosophise on different topics.

"Nothing is left of our noble traditions. Let me tell you how I married my Mary. The Cossacks from the Trans-Baikal Region had a tradition, whereby a fiancé had to show his bravery and dexterity to his intended bride. I was dancing with my intended at the bride show *(a gathering of families to assess the suitability of the prospective bride and groom MH),* and she and I were circling each other. She was holding a handkerchief and I-a drawn sword. She was holding her cambric hankie by two corners and was twisting it around in front of her face. I turned around and -hey presto! -slashed it into two halves. Keep in mind that

I did not cut it in front of me, which is simple, but over the back of my head! Should I have misjudged the movement, she could have lost her arm or had her face disfigured; do you get the danger? It is frightening to think about it now... But that's how it was in those days: she was not allowed to be frightened, and I had to be brave or get the hell out of her life. However, we practiced trick riding since childhood and I was able to slash a piece of vine in half whilst riding on a galloping horse with an accuracy of two inches (*the measure quoted in the story is the Russian "Vershok", equal to about two inches MH*). Be as it may, I did not bring shame upon myself, but cut her handkerchief in half whilst she was holding it in her hands! That's how my Maria Grigoryevna became my wife! We have been happily married for a quarter of a century now and have grown sons, but God only knows whether I'll ever see them again..."

Starting from 1949 the Gulag camps of the Chaun-Chukotsk Industrial Region of Dalstroy ("*Far Eastern Construction Concern*" in *Russian MH*) had to finance their own existence and the prisoners started getting wages. The pay was miserly, but it allowed one a chance to buy a couple of loaves of bread, a handful of sugar, a cake of soap or a packet of makhorka in the camp store. I was still imprisoned when the first wages were given out, but my share was handed over by mistake to my one and only namesake, and much to my chagrin I was unable to rectify that error. However, Peter collected his wages and showed me his money. The first sight of that money seemed to me to represent an unattainable happiness, as they represented a chance to buy something other than the oatmeal porridge mixed with chaff, which I was utterly bored with for the rest of my life. I was looking at his banknotes with great respect, but he tossed them irreverently into the air, clearly saying in his flat voice:

"Is this supposed to be money? No, it is just paper! Real money is the one, which can be exchanged for gold! Who is going to give gold for this stuff! Paper –that's all it is!"

Our friendship lasted for several years, with a few interruptions. However, Pyotr was not destined to return from Chukotka, and neither was his Mariya Grigoryevna able to see her husband again. I attended the Cossack's funeral as an ex-prisoner in 1954. At that time he had been working as a store manager in a mining settlement called Youzhny *("Southern" in Russian MH)* and died in his sleep of a heart attack. He left me a fabulous wristwatch of a make called "Pobeda" *("Victory"in Russian MH)*, which he chose by listening to the sound made by the mechanisms of a shipment of watches, and which lasted me for 33 years.

During my first winter at Chukotka most ordinary prisoners wore footwear named "bakhils", which was made from the sleeves of old winter coats attached to pieces of used tyres. Those contraptions tended to slip off one's feet and their upturned toes made them reminiscent of ancient Dutch or Turkish moccasins. I used to walk along the aisles of our hut to the accompaniment of a chorus of jokes from the wittier crims:

CHAPTER 6

"How do you like your ballroom shoes, landowner? How do you like the Soviet Government? You would have never been able to afford such luxury had it not been for its benevolence!"

How did these characters know about my past? My whole past, my nearest and dearest were lost in some kind of a fog and were almost abstract entities. The main thing was to survive till tomorrow and, most importantly, to have something to eat. The arctic winters in the camp seemed to last forever, particularly for those of us who had to work underground. Daylight lasting barely for four hours started and ended quite imperceptibly. I was lucky to see a star at the beginning or end of a shift. Mostly, however, all one saw was a dull grey sky with small boring snowflakes constantly falling from it. The snow-drifts kept growing as well as did white mounds of snow, looking like giant hats, on the roofs of the prison huts. The barbed wire surrounding the barracks in several densely packed rows reminded me of Christmas decorations. It used to always vibrate as if it were shaking from a horrible fright... I used to leave the putrid hut in the middle of the night to get a breath of fresh air and look with fascination at the inexplicable dance of the barbed wire, but could never understand its cause. It was perhaps due to the electric current circulating through it, or to the magnetic field of the Earth.

During rare clear nights I could not stop admiring the orange dancing lights of the Northern Aurora I saw in the distance, which forever changed their brightness. That was a fairytale picture!

Frightening snowstorms would blow in the second half of winter. They were so fierce that on occasions one could not see one's own outstretched arm. A rope was connected between the hut and the dining room on such days and a detachment of slave labourers and perished together with its guards. They were found many days later under snow, which was quite hard by then. The only thing that led the rescuers to their burial spot was the sight of a man's arm sticking out above the snow.

We were forced to go to work the moment the snowstorm became less fierce and walked in formation under the supervision of the guards. The wind would pierce my jacket and warm vest reaching all the way to my bones and burn my frostbitten nose and cheeks. I used to protect my face with torn sleeves of my jacket, but was not able to bend, let alone step to the side, mindful of the "morning prayer" read to us before the commencement of a march: "One step left, one step right— we'll shoot without warning!" Any slave labourer who slipped, fell and rolled to the side used to receive "nine grams of lead" in those days, and forever stay on the side of the track, whereas the guard got a citation for bravery, a monetary reward and sometimes even an extra holiday...

Our work in the mines was meant to be done by horses. We used to load the ore, which had been blasted by the miners into iron barrels which had been cut lengthwise in half and put on sleds and drag them to a large bunker located one or two hundred metres away, for delivery to the top of the mine. The floor of the mine was supposed to have been sprinkled with snow, but that requirement was often ignored and we dragged the ore along a stone-covered path. The lighting consisted of widely spaced dull lamps made of a wick placed in a tin containing some motor oil. Two men would drag the load attached to a cable, with a timber board placed on their shoulders, like a beam usually placed on a horse's back, with the third one pushing from behind. They were supervised by six foremen, the worst representatives of the criminal scum who were ingratiating themselves with the authorities, waving their sticks and shouting: "Get on with it– move, you bastards!" There was no one to protect the slaves. Such a system suited the authorities who covertly encouraged it.

"How about taking this low life on a hunt for a tiger, bear or even a wild pig?"–thought I–"They would have most certainly needed a change of underwear after such an experience, whereas here I, a tiger hunter, and other strong men have to give in to those drags of humanity."

But my thoughts notwithstanding, I had to breathe in the soot from the wicks of the oil lamps and cough it up all night in the hut.

We worked without any holidays, with snowstorms being our only hope, but the food was nothing like the fare needed by a miner. All we were given was a scoop of fish head soup and a scoop of oat porridge with chaff whose taste I got to hate for the rest of my days. I still cannot understand why the Gulag bosses had to save money on feeding the prisoners. After all, they brought them to the mines from heaven knows how far away and these mostly young men could have produced a decent output if they were decently and humanely fed. The camp where I found myself was not one of the death camps for the so-called "enemies of the people"—a miserable crowd of people wearing prison numbers on their clothes, who were deliberately, albeit slowly exterminated. That was not the case with us, as we belonged to a system of Chun-Chukotsk gulags under the management of "Dalnostroy" ("*Far Eastern Development Corporation" in Russian MH*), which was involved in the mining of tin, a metal badly needed by the Government. However, absence of vitamins and calories quickly killed us off.

Once every ten days we were taken to a bathhouse where one was forced to look at naked bodies, and I could never get used to that frightening sight. All one saw were skin and bones, with the skin covered in sores. Many men developed dystrophy. Their necks were frighteningly thin, the ribs and shoulder blades were sticking out, and elbows and knees looked like billiard balls. They had no bottoms and the space between their legs looked like an oval window.

A vicious epidemic of scurvy set in towards the beginning of spring. Dark spots would appear on a man's body, which turned into rotting ulcers, cramps would twist his arms and legs and he developed palpitations. Some people used to extract or spit loose teeth out of their mouths whilst having breakfast or dinner at filthy tables in the canteen. I used to massage my gums every morning using either salt or simply the index finger, and saved my front teeth as a result. However, many scurvy sufferers did not survive their condition and left this world with a token stating their name tied around one leg...

I could still walk but could no longer run and looked with envy at sprightly well-fed criminal "bitches", thinking to myself: "It was not long ago when I could jump around just like they".

Barrels of a scurvy medicine consisting of an extract of a dwarf Arctic cedar were delivered to the camp. The inmates were lined up after returning from work and given a table spoon of that thick brown and intolerably bitter liquid, which proved to be a miraculous cure. Almost all of the survivors of the epidemic who partook of it on a daily basis recovered and never again contracted scurvy. The extract seemed to act like some sort of a vaccine. (Actually, it corrected a serious vitamin deficiency. ES)

However, there were some who lost all hope for the future and continued the acts of self harm for the purpose of being declared medically unfit and returned to the mainland. One evening a quiet hard working and seemingly uncomplaining prisoner found a Bickford safety fuse and cap in the work area, hid it in his felt boot and brought it back with him to the camp. We were all crowded at the entrance to our hut when he lit the fuse and shouted: "Don't go near me, I am about to blow up!"—and rushed into a timber toilet full of frozen human excreta, which suddenly shook and lit up with a crimson flame. Its door was blown off and the victim fell out with a terrible scream. One of his legs had been blown off below the knee. He was picked up and continued screaming while being dragged away to an unknown destination.

Two others committed suicide in a similar manner when they lost at cards, which they knew meant an inevitable execution. They wrapped Bickford fuses around their necks, lit them and had their heads blown off.

It was obvious to me that only a fool would attempt to escape from Chukotka and I immediately abandoned any plans in that direction, although I kept thinking of an escape before we arrived in Pevek. It was an impossible thing north of the Arctic Circle. The tundra stretched in all directions and icy impassable rivers and swarms of midges (gnatlike insects) made the task impossible in Summer. The Winters were cold, there were frequent snow drifts, and the snow-covered tundra was like a desert. It was impossible to obtain any foodstuffs without weapons, and, besides, one would always leave visible tracks on the snow. The Chukcha hunters were an additional hazard as they were paid a premium for the murder of would-be escapees.

This having said, some inmates continued to try to escape. A prisoner asked a guard for a light and taking advantage of the young lad's inexperience, grabbed his rifle and stabbed him to death with its bayonet. A few men left with that man, but they were all captured with the aid of guard dogs and killed. One of the victims was a thief by the name of Sashka, whom I knew from Nakhodka where I was helping him to write love letters to his "golden-locked" belle.

Five men escaped from our hut in winter, which caused me some trouble, as they stole my fur hat and my pride and joy—a pair of pinkish valenki (felt boots). I was silly enough to report my losses and our camp boss decided that I had helped with the escape and told the camp accountant to charge me for the lost property, which cost me several hundred roubles and which took me a whole year to pay off.

Four fugitives were quickly found and killed and their frozen bloodied and twisted bodies were brought to the camp and thrown under the barbed wire surrounding our compound as a deterrent to would-be escapees. Their frightful bodies "adorned" that spot for a few days. As far as the fifth member of the escape party was concerned, he was a young naïve and inexperienced fellow and served as a source of meat for the rest of the group. The soldiers who conducted the operation returned his hacked up body to the camp in a canvas bag. It was rumoured that part of one of his arms had been chopped off, baked on a fire and eaten in the cave, where the rest of the escapees had been captured.

Later captured escapees used to be taken outside, stripped naked and hosed down till they stopped moving. We were marched past those unfortunates and we were told not to look in their direction, but we used to peek at the victims who were sitting and crawling on the snow looking like tree stumps under the merciless stream of water from the hoses directed at them...

Hunger was getting to us, which forced us to deliver water to the kitchen at the end of a 12-hour shift to earn additional rations. We worked in the dark, covered in a layer of ice, using our last resources, but fat cooks demanded an additional trip before giving us any food. Once they cheated us and left before serving us our "pay", after which we swore not to kill ourselves for them again. Luckily, I was able to find another job with the camp bursar, which consisted of dressing of deer hides for the manufacture of mattresses and bedding and spent nearly a month "loafing" in the camp. My job consisted of covering the raw side of the hides with bran and scratching off the layer of fat. My assistants and I used to make flat cakes out of leftover bran and bake them with the smelly fat of marine creatures, which was also used as part of the dressing process. However, that job was soon over and I had to return to the mine.

...One night our detachment staggered wearily into our hut, which was lit with a strong lamp. Our foreman, a "bitch" (criminal) by the name of Kolka Cherkas, was sitting in the far corner of the room on a heap of pillows and blankets covered in colourful cases, in company of "sixes" and "mistresses"– good-looking young fellows with female nicknames. He saw me and waved his hand:

"Listen, the URCH *(A Russian acronym for "The Placement Branch" MH)* people are looking for you. Get there on the double! I wonder what they have dreamt up? Hurry anyway—they say it's urgent. Let me know later what's going on."

A visit to the URCH never bode well. I was hungry and dirty, but immediately trudged along to their office, knocked on the door, entered and reported standing to attention, as required by the Gulag rules: "Prisoner Yankovsky, convicted in accordance with article so and so, so many years imprisonment. Here as requested by you." A young rosy-cheeked supervising officer sitting behind a brightly lit desk looked me up from head to toe and after a pregnant pause uttered condescendingly through clenched teeth:

"Come to the table and sign this!"

I felt weak. Why? I was not aware of any misdemeanours on my part. The young man appeared to have understood my anxiety and smiled:

"Don't be afraid. This time there is something favourable for you."– He took an official-looking document out of a folder and read it aloud, without giving it to me:

"In accordance with the decision of the Military Commission of the Supreme Court, the sentence in accordance with Article 58/14 –'escape and counter-revolutionary sabotage' to be reclassified to Article 82, part 1, and as a result of that to change the sentence from twenty five to three years...."

I kind of understood the words, but could not believe them, and everything appeared to be swimming before my eyes. The officer explained:

"You have already served a few years, which leaves you a total of about nine to go. It should be possible to send you to work without a guard. That's all. Go and have some rest now."

That was the first pleasant news after all those years! I returned to the hut, still not fully comprehending what had happened to my life. I did remember, however, that after I had been sentenced in Ussuriysk to 25 years hard labour I requested a piece of paper and a pencil when I found out that prisoners were allowed to object to their sentences within 72 hours of their pronouncement and wrote an appeal in capital letters because my cell was practically dark. In that appeal I tried to explain to some unknown official what happened in my life and why. I did it just in case because I did not believe in my chances of success.

Well, and there I was. It was obvious that even in those frightening times just people were not completely extinct. Somebody read my plea, somebody else went into the circumstances of my case, somebody concurred with the conclusion and yet another somebody signed and approved the recommendation...

No guard! How can anybody who never experienced my travails understand my exhilaration? I was so used to walk as one of a group of five slaves, to listen to the shouts "one step left, one step right—I'll shoot without warning!" that I could not comprehend that I was walking alone and could, if I wanted to take a step to the right or to the left? And I did test that newly acquired freedom, which gave me an indescribable joy. I don't know whether such a pastime can be described as fun, but if it can, then my life became easier.

My new job was that of a carrier of soup, a task, which I had performed in Vanino some time ago. An assistant and I had to carry the soup to all the huts in the camp, which naturally meant that we could help ourselves to a thicker liquid from the bottom of the barrel. Amazing as it may sound, during the next or, perhaps, the one after next, visit to the bathhouse I noticed that my body became rounder and my skin became more supple. It seems that a healthy body does not need much to recover, provided, of course, one is still basically healthy.

My next assignment was that of a timekeeper and later still as an economist. What constitutes the "aristocracy" of a prison camp? On the territory of the camp "aristocrats" are the bursar, the storeman, the bookkeeper and the cooks, whereas in the mine they were the foremen and office workers. The foremen, who mostly came from the criminal elements, were often illiterate and therefore bookkeepers, economists and people who set production quotas were the leading "aristocracy" in the field.

I remember that my uncle always said that two periods dominate a man's life: a black and a red one. It seems that 1949 was the beginning of my red period.

A mining engineer 1st class, a skinny and wiry free man by the name of Dashkovsky, was charge of our mine. He was very polite, reserved and, unlike the other free men, never swore at the prisoners. On the contrary, he spoke nicely and used a "you" instead of "thou" when addressing one of us. He used to talk to us in his office located under a hill near a small river and made me feel like a free man. During one of his friendly chats he mentioned that his son failed English in the sixth year of Primary School and had to sit for a deferred examination. He needed a tutor, but where can one find such a person in this environment? One of the clerks pointed towards me: "Here you are. Yankovsky used to live abroad and could perhaps help you." Dashkovsky beamed:

"Will you be able to coach my lad? We still have two months before the test. I can get you permission to come to my house after work, if you are willing to give it a go."

He did get me that permission, and for the first time after several years I crossed the threshold of a private home, actually a family hut covered in white paint. In that primitive flat I was introduced to the engineer's teenage son and friendly wife. She immediately invited me to have a meal consisting of bread and homemade and *schi* (*cabbage soup* MH), the taste of which I had almost forgotten. Yes, I am telling the truth! At the end of the first lesson I took half a loaf of bread with me to give to my mates, but it was confiscated at the gate by the guards. "You must have pinched it in the village'—said they. That assignment gave new life, whereas not such a long time ago I was sure that I was going to die without ever having a fill of black bread.

It has to be said that I earned my bread at Dashkovskys because the lad passed his exam.

In 1950 I was transferred to another camp together with a large group of other inmates. It was a smaller establishment near the Head Office of the "Krasnoarmeyskaya" mine. I was sad to leave behind my old OLP mates, and particularly missed Kvasov.

Several prisoners were working in the Head Office and I was also offered a position, which involved the permission of the head of the OLP major Mikhailov. I wrote an application and gave it to the head of the Planning Department who passed it on to Mikhailov, who wrote on it in red pencil: PERMISSION DENIED. I was a former fugitive, albeit working without supervision by a guard, and as such had a red line drawn diagonally across my papers. People like me were classified as dangerous and used to be locked up as precaution during the public holidays of the First of May and the October Day (*anniversary of the Communist revolution in Russia MH*). I was one of those unfortunates.

However, it is an ill wind, which blows nobody any good. The authorities introduced a bonus for good work. For example, camp assistants had half a day taken off each month of their remaining sentence, and field workers were given a whole two days, provided they managed to achieve an output equal to at least 121% of the required quota. Consequently, a model worker received a reduction of a whole three days per month of the remaining sentence! My previous sentence was due to expire in 1972, but the new date was 1957, which included the reduced sentence for my escape. By strange coincidence, 1957 was the date of my total exoneration "due to the absence of criminally punishable conduct", which was announced to me at the KGB Headquarters when I was already a free settler in the city of Magadan...

In the meantime, a light at the end of a long tunnel appeared to me in that camp. I realised that it was possible with a bit of luck to reduce my remaining sentence to about three years. I found out that that was possible, provided I got a job with the GRB (*a Russian acronym for "Mining Research Bureau" MH*). The job involved obtaining samples of ore from the mine or its surface. The samples were then washed in water contained in heated tanks, dried and blasted with air, which produced a pure concentrate, which enabled a geologist to determine the quantity of metal in a given area of the mine. The work was hard, but it was lucrative, as one day was counted for three!

I soon became a foreman and a right hand man of the site geologist by the name of Nikolay Petrovich Lobushin. Looking back, I think that he was an ex-prisoner or an exile, although he never mentioned that fact. He did, however, told me once, after we had a furtive drink of pure spirit mixed with water in one of the huts belonging to the GRB, that his parents belonged to the nobility.

Political prisoners served their time alongside ordinary criminals in the camps of "Dalnostroy", but free workers treated them differently. When people like myself met educated people amongst the administration, they were met with trust and compassion, although they did not dare openly show it, as it was not only against the rules, but also quite dangerous. The MGB *(a former name of the KGB MH)* had two distinct categories of prisoners: professional criminals, who were classified as friends, regardless of the crime they had committed, and political prisoners –all of whom were known as "enemies of the people." If a free worker was seen to be friendly with an "enemy", his career, and worse, were placed in jeopardy.

However, there was a continuous struggle for our services. Business people saw reliable workers and assistants in political prisoners and tried to help them get jobs, but met with constant obstruction from the camp authorities, which sent them their men, i.e. the criminal "friends of the people," but they were only employable as messengers or cleaners.

The crims behaved insolently, openly calling Stalin a "shoe-shiner" because his father was a cobbler, or "a moustache" and openly cursed him, loudly laughing at their own jokes, but got away with that conduct. Had an unguarded word been pronounced by a "counterrevolutionary", the snitches would have immediately reported him to the officer in charge of the camp, and there would have been hell to pay. It was not unusual to have one's sentence increase as a result of such a happening. The dark shadow of Lavrenty Pavlovich Beria (*the chief of the KGB MH*) hung over the heads of the "enemies of the people" even in the faraway Chukotsk tundra...

Stalin's fateful dictum about the "intensification of the class struggle" embodied in the statement: "if the enemy does not surrender, he must be exterminated" produced a feeling of intense hate towards the victims of Article 58 of the penal code (*dealing with political prisoners MH)* in the members of the MGB *(later KGB MH)*. I am sure that major Mikhailov understood full well that no clear thinking person would attempt to escape from Chukotka, but was physically incapable of allowing any concessions to me, a former émigré. He loved his power of refusing all my applications with a curt note "Declined—Mikhailov." I am sure that he could have never imagined that I would be rehabilitated and that we would meet on equal terms in a supermarket queue in Magadan. But meet we did. I chanced to look around and saw a portly red-faced individual in a lambskin jacket without shoulder straps standing behind me. His pale bulging eyes became quite round.

Chapter 6

"—Oh, it is *thou (an insulting way of addressing a subordinate in Russian MH)* ....you....I am glad..." stammered he.

It seems that encounters of that kind were quite uncomfortable for Mikhailov, who left the queue without making a purchase and beat a hasty retreat from the shop. I presume that some of his former victims did not exercise the same exemplary restraint as I...

Chapter 7: The Last Camp

Here I was again: a new "home", new faces. It is very sad to lose touch with one's friends and is particularly so in the prison environment, when the loss of a mate again throws one into the unknown, feeling like a dry twig in the murky stream of life.

Summers are short north of the Arctic Circle. It is full of storms, rain and even snowfalls, but, nevertheless, there is a growth of grass and of pale practically scentless flowers. However, August can be warm, dark blue and even golden, followed by snow on the hills, in the yard, on the roofs of the prison huts and on the several rows of barbed wire. The sun disappears between November and February, but the sky turns pale pink in the morning giving birth to a grey day, soon to be followed by night, which starts at four in the afternoon.

All that having said, as a result of my experiences in the camp, I was no longer a "rotten intellectual". I did not have an official title, but was already enjoying some authority as an economist, a technician in charge of assaying of the ore and a foreman.

Birds of a feather flock together in a camp, and I joined a group of four similar individuals. We used to meet in the camp barbershop, which was owned by an Armenian by the name Ter–Ovasenyan. The others were a bulldozer operator by the name of Arkady Kuankov, who was a Korean half-cast and a native of the town of Khabarovsk, a Georgian by the name of Georgii Arsenidze, who was a former lieutenant-captain of the Black Sea Fleet, and yours truly. Arsenidze was in charge of a mining gallery, which were referred to as "mines". All of us dined together. I have already mentioned that the inmates of camps always tried to get extra rations and share them with their mates. Some of us worked without supervision by guards, whereas others, though supervised, worked with free men. All of us used to be given an assignment to visit the Head Office, which gave the opportunity to duck out to a store, provided the supervisors weren't looking, and buy a tin of canned meat, tea, sugar or butter. These items invariably found their way into the barbershop, where we spent most of our evenings after finishing work.

Seryozha *(a diminutive form of the Russian name "Sergei" MH)* Ter-Ovasenyan used to work in the Siberian town of Sverdlovsk at a factory called "Uralmash" as a specialist in the area of thermal treatment of metals, but had never severed his ties with his native Armenia. He was proud of his homeland and insisted that the famous Georgian poem "Knight in a Tiger's Skin" was written by an Armenian.

"What is the meaning of the prefix 'Ter' in my surname?'—would he ask rhetorically.—"It means that some members of our clan belonged to the clergy, see?"

Statements of that kind were quite daring in those days.

The youngest member of our group was the Korean half-cast Arkasha (*a diminutive form of the Russian name "Arkady" MH*) Kuankov who worked as a bulldozer operator in the mechanical workshop of our mine and, having been born in Khabarovsk, was like me, a native of the Far East. His mother had for many years been an editor of a paper called "Tikhookeanskaya Zvezda" (*"The Star of the Pacific Ocean" MH*), and Arkasha was the only member of our group who received occasional letters from home.

Arsenidze was a skinny but wiry Georgian who had no ties with his homeland and had, perhaps, as a condition of his sentence, no right of correspondence. He was a former Communist and had a ferocious hatred of Beria (The Chief of the KGB).

He was an ambitious and proud man who had high ideals and worked like a man possessed, not sparing his strength, even in captivity. Any break down at work would upset Arsenidze, but he was happy like a child when things went well. The work quota ("plan") was his life and he used to work an extra half a shift in the event of problems with the plan, often getting wet and cold. He finally caught a bad cold and had to stay away from work. He was constantly coughing and getting worse by the hour. Soon he was no longer able to visit the barber shop and asked me to visit his hut and tell him about the goings on in the mine.

I would sit on his bed near his feet, and Arsenidze used to suddenly sit up, when our mine was mentioned during the news bulletin, point to the loud speaker hanging on the wall and say:

"Just listen! Listen about my mine! These layabouts have again mucked up the 'plan'! Wait till I get better and go back there"...

He did not get better, but quickly died of galloping consumption, that brave Captain-Lieutenant who died two months before the demise of his personal enemy Beria. In accordance with the rules of those days, his naked purple and twisted body was handed over to us from the morgue. Arkasha and I put Arsenidze's body on a sleigh and buried it at the bottom of a hill, not forgetting to tie a wooden label around his ankle. We did all we could to mark his grave: we collected a few wind-swept stones and placed them atop the snow-covered mound above his last resting place....

Happiness and sorrow are inevitable in life, just as the presence of friends and foes. This is particularly true in a camp, where a helping shoulder of a mate is absolutely vital. However, life often upsets our plans. Luybushkin went on holidays and his temporary replacement was a lazy drunkard, a young member of the Komsomol *(Communist Youth Organisation MH)*, by the name of Terekhov, who fell victim to the poisonous influence of the criminal element. These people used to steal metal produced by the other prisoners, sell it to the Government, pretending it to be the result of labours of the free workers, and shared the proceeds with Terekhov, to avoid detection and punishment. That was a criminal offence, which exposed the weakness of the new boss, as the old one would have never condoned it.

I was not aware of Terekhov's complicity and told him about the scam in order to save him from punishment, but this cad reported me to the professional criminals. Their despicable leader by the name of Rasskazov sent against me a powerfully-built thug with a nickname "Tushonka" (*"Bacon" MH*) who ambushed me between the bunks, but I managed to kick him away and jumped on him in the middle of the hut. However, I noticed that his mates were preparing a counter-attack with the aid of an iron rod. I beat a hasty retreat and spent the night in the barber shop. I did not leave my job but started to carry a piece of a rubber hose hidden in my felt boot, meant as a weapon against the thugs. The crooks were sacked after the return of Luybushkin from his leave.

Once, when, climbing out of the mine, I saw a skinny fellow carrying a heavy bag of ore desperately trying to climb a staircase hacked out of frozen ground. He seemed to be crying. The lad gave me a sad look and said:

"I can't climb the stairs with this heavy bag"...

He was a new inmate whom I had already seen around and knew that his name was Sasha P. who came from Moscow. I helped him with the heavy load, which was beyond the physical capabilities of the starving youth, and we became better acquainted with each other. Some time later I managed to get Sasha a job as a mine-surveyor whose duties involved carrying around a surveyor's rod, which was well within his capabilities. Our lives went their separate ways soon after that, but I did meet him 28 years later! Sasha found my name in the magazine called "Okhota" *("The Hunters' Magazine" in Russian MH)*, called me on the phone and we agreed to meet at the entrance to a Moscow underground *("Metro")* station called "Vernadsky Prospect". My friend turned into an imposing well-dressed gentleman with greying temples. Sasha was accompanied by his seven-year granddaughter whom he affectionately held by the hand.

Several economists from the ranks of prisoners were involved in the creation of the production plan for 1951, even though the camp administration was opposed to the idea. However, they stipulated that the political prisoners would work at night, i.e. after the end of the official working day, so as to prevent them, God forbid, from "an attempt to politically corrupt the free employees...."

About five of us sat at separate tables in the spacious office of the Chief Engineer. The grateful free workers supplied us not only with the necessary tools of trade, such as rulers, abacuses, paper, pens and pencils, but also a couple of loaves of bread, about ten salted herrings and a few packets of tea, which was extremely rare in the camp, because it was used for the preparation of a brew called "chifir."

Chifir is made from tea leaves, which are boiled in a closed vessel containing very little water. For example, a 300 gram can of chifir requires one packet of tea. It is an incredibly bitter drink, which produces a constricting feeling in the mouth, but it produces a feeling akin to intoxication or rather of excitement, which induces sleeplessness. I tried the taste of chifir on my tongue before that night, but never drank it.

Jenka Janiev, a foul-mouthed drunkard and gambler, but a remarkably quick and capable bookkeeper, was our chifir expert. I got to know him when I started my career as an area timekeeper subordinate to an economist. A tipsy Jenka decided to "teach me a lesson". He found a mistake in one of my entries and started abusing me:

"Are you cooking the records? Are you demanding bribes from the workers for adding fictitious times to their claims? I'll tear off your head for that!..."

The other people sitting around the table held their breath. "Will Jenka cower the 'new boy' and force him to do his bidding, or won't he?" -thought they."

It is possible that I would have been taken aback in the past, but by that time I had enough experience in a prison camp. I leaned over the table and quietly and distinctly said among a deathly silence, looking Jenka straight in the eye:

"Listen, Janiev, one more word and you will turn very pale. You would wish that there was a fifth corner in this room where you could hide."

The crowd giggled approvingly, and Janiev got the message and shut up.

Getting back to the story, we nearly finished the drafting of the production plan by 1am. The papers were put away into the safe, and food appeared on the desks, which were covered with some newspapers. Janiev was working away on the chifir and I quickly put away a whole fat herring, which made my innards burn with salt. I went to the toilet and upon my return found a half litre tin of a strangely cloudy tea sitting in front of my place, which I gulped down in one hit, initially experiencing only its extreme bitterness. The others did not say anything but sat with open mouths while I was gulping down the chifir. We got dressed and repaired for our camp, which was a kilometre down the road. The temperature outside was close to minus forty degrees and my mates lowered the flaps of their fur hats and started to button up their coats, but I felt strangely hot, unbuttoned my coat, took off my hat and did not put it on during the whole journey. I laid down on my bunk after getting back, but was unable to sleep all night and my heart was racing like after a long run. That was the last time in my life that I drank chifir.

Shortly after Arsenidze's death in the spring of 1951 I started feeling very sick. I had pains in my side and under a shoulder blade and found it painful to sleep on the back. In addition to that, I felt apathetic and sluggish. Was it TB? Did I catch the infection from my pal when I was sitting on his bunk? I was nearing forty, the critical time of life, which had been predicted to me in the Khabarovsk prison by the old Korean fortune-teller!

The sad thing was that my life was getting easier. Time was when I did not know whether I would live another day and all my strength was directed towards survival and I rarely thought of my family. It sounds terrible, but that is the truth. Yet now that I knew that I should be able to survive, I suddenly started thinking of my wife and son. How are they? Are they safe and sound? Or are they starving to death? Where are my father and my brothers and sisters? Mum was lucky, as she died in 1936 and was buried in Korea...

I understood that if I did not overcome the condition prophesied to me by the soothsayer I would perish. I cannot describe how hard I had to summon all my will to battle the depression, but I overcame it and was my former healthy self by that summer.

It was the beginning of the ore enrichment season, various machines were making a huge din producing tin from the ore, which had been accumulated during the winter operations of the mine. However, in addition to tin there were also minute quantities of gold, which was mostly consisted of small grains, but there were also occasional nuggets. The mine workers used to find small nuggets during the washing of samples of ore and sometimes came across them directly in the mines.

The metal is collected at the end of a shift when the machinery is no longer working. After the refinement of the ore, tin is automatically fed towards the far end of a hollow trough, but I noticed that after the metal was removed from the trough, a group of crafty prisoners would gather at its near end and fossick for something, dip their finger into the trough and put it in their mouth. It turned out that they were picking up grains of gold. They could not officially sell it and the mere act of its collection was considered a crime punishable by extra imprisonment. Why then did these unfortunates take such risks? The answer was simple: there were shortages of everything: bread, sugar, tea, but shortage of tobacco was the worst of all, which produced a black market in that product. I personally saw hanging on the wall of our Head Office an instruction from the Manager, which stated that anybody who found a piece of a bulldozer drive chain, fallen off a machine, would be rewarded with a...joint of makhorka! The craving for tobacco was so strong that men would lug these pieces, weighing several kilograms each, through mud and slush to the office to collect their smoke..

That's how men were legally rewarded for parts of bulldozers, but grains of gold were taken to the foremen or the camp storeman, where they were also exchanged for makhorka. These individuals put the tiny pieces of gold into little bottles, hoping to smuggle them out of the camp after the expiration of their sentence and to sell them on the mainland, although that, as mentioned, was a punishable offence. Sashka Chipizubov, the camp storeman, established a price for gold, which would have made the old hands of Klondike gold rushes proud: a gram of gold for a gram of makhorka! And, would you believe, the prisoners hid their finds of gold from the guards as best they could and took them to Sashka!

Life was not getting any better in the camp. We were undergoing frequent searches. A so-called "complete search" involved all prisoners being marched outside to wait in the snow while all our belonging left in the hut were turned upside down and inside out. Searched were our beds, bedside tables, and every nook and cranny where inmates could have hidden homemade knives, blades, and anything else that could have been made in a smithy or on a lathe. All suspicious items were confiscated so as to thwart a possible escape or armed attack on the guards.

The criminal element among us used to smuggle alcohol into the camp. In addition to that it was possible to obtain alcohol from the prison hospital. The camp medical orderly called Karpenko used to save the fiery liquid and organise parties. I remember coming to one of them late, tired and hungry and, in accordance with the touching Russian custom to force latecomers to have a stiff drink, being given a full tumbler of pure alcohol, which I had to skol, again in accordance with an age-old tradition! I was silly enough to down the drink on an empty stomach and immediately passed out. I slept on the floor under the hospital table till the morning reveille, when Karpenko had to shake me awake at the sight of a blinking lamp and the sound of an iron rod hitting the rail outside our hut.

I thought that I was going to be an object of universal ridicule, but far from it: the foremen were exhilarated. They concealed the incident from the authorities and told me: "That's the boy! We are very proud of you!" My drunken stupor turned me into a hero in their eyes.

We had another unwritten rule in the camp, that of feasting important people. Being first an Area Economist and later an assay technician, I joined the camp elite. Why?—Because my reports largely determined the percentage composition of metal in the ore of various sections of the mine, which, in turn, decided whether they had met their production targets.

Each large production unit was located in a separate hut and their powerful leaders used to invite the generally despised but important political prisoners to their receptions. Invited were the accountant, the person in charge of the setting of production targets, the economist, the mine technician–in other words all of those who could be useful to them. As a result of that, we, the "politicals", found ourselves in company of the camp "aristocracy"–such men as Kadyrov, Cherkasov, Shadrinsky and others.

The foremen lived in a hut with double bunks, reminiscent of a train with sleeping berths, and their compartment was separated from the rest of the room with Government-issue bed sheets. These bosses were always surrounded by their cronies and "girls'–cute-looking young fellows with nicknames like Sonka, Mashka, Dashka etc *(Note:"Sonka", for example, is a diminutive of a girl's name "Sonya" MH)*. The bosses were wealthy. Next to a bed table of such an individual one found open tins of Russian beef and American sausages and frankfurters–leftovers of American supplies under the Lend-Lease arrangements during WWII. Thick slices of bread were lying about and jars with pure alcohol and water stood on the table. The visitors mixed alcohol with water according to individual tastes: some used a mixture of one third alcohol with two thirds water, and others took their drinks fifty-fifty. The mixture would initially "boil" –i.e. turn cloudy, but soon turned clear again.

CHAPTER 7

Drinking and eating usually took place in turns, because spirits were customarily drunk from one glass, which was shaken free of the remnants of liquid before passing it on. The idea was not to use too much crockery to avoid drawing attention of the guards. Another precaution was to have look-outs from the "sixes'—bosses' stooges—posted near the entrance to the hut, but I think that these thugs managed to bribe the guards, and there usually was no danger from them.

The party consisted of a friendly chat intermingled with jokes and funny stories. Nobody said a word about business, as everybody understood the purpose of the gathering, and we all religiously observed the camp etiquette.

However, a reception of this kind did not rely only on food and banter—it required a theatrical performance. An essential part of this part was the showing off of a boss's underlings. I remember how the feared leader of the thugs, a well-built handsome Tartar by the name of Kadyrov, gave a sign to the guests, which announced the beginning of such a performance. What was the performance about? Well, we all drink diluted alcohol, but the members of his "six" (*bodyguards*) drink pure alcohol on an empty stomach!

"Look!"– says Kadyrov and nudges a vassal who is, or pretends to be, asleep under a blanket on a nearby bunk. The lad sits up and rubs his eyes. Kadyrov points to a glass filled to the brim with pure alcohol. "Well—go for it!"

The fellow nods, takes the glass and downs it without saying a word. He then wipes his mouth with the fist, goes back to his bunk and pulls the sheet over his head, without even looking at the food.

"What do you think of my heroes?!" proudly exclaims Kadyrov, looking at his guests. We look at each other and act suitably impressed. And what about the "hero" under the blanket? One can only imagine his condition. He is burning inside and is craving for a drink of water. However, that would destroy the theatrical effect of the performance and the boss would lose his prestige, which, in turn, would mean that the current six hangers on would lose the cushy position of court jesters.

That was the internal picture of life in the camp. But what about the male "mistresses"? They arrogantly gaze at others from underneath the boss's blanket. They are the untouchables! Many of them get exempted from work because of their position, although they rarely keep their positions for long. New recruits are always chosen from the newly arrived prisoners. The discarded "used" courtesans are the subject of vile gossip around the camp, and are said to exude a revolting smell, real or imagined.

Another large group of prisoners arrived at the end of summer 1951. They had all been convicted under Article 58 of the penal code. It seems that new "mass political crimes" had been discovered in Russia. The seasoned inmates of the camp surrounded the new arrivals after the guards who delivered them went away. "Well, what is it like in the 'Big Smoke?'" -they wanted to know.

CHAPTER 7

A large fellow, who was still in a reasonable physical condition, stepped forward. He looked just like a character from a famous picture "The Zaporozhye Cossacks Are Writing a Letter to the Turkish Sultan." With one leg theatrically thrust forward and gesticulating with his arms, he announced:

"The Big Smoke? Well, it is a complete haymaking! Everybody is getting a short haircut. Devil alone knows what's going on!"...

Winters are depressing north of the Arctic Circle. It is dark, cold, and snowing, but the Sun does not set at all in Summer. It is red and floats above the tundra and the sea. One wakes up not knowing whether it is four am or pm. However, man gets used to it. But the midges are a horse of a different colour... Their attacks during calm days drive you mad. Midges swarm like a black cloud and get into one's eyes, nose, find their ways under the sleeves behind the collar of a shirt, stinging mercilessly all the time. It is impossible to get used to it. Free workers were saved by the use of ointments or nets, which, however, were often very stuffy. Alas, the prisoners were not issued with nets and there was no one higher up they could complain about the torment they were undergoing.

A large column of prisoners containing several working teams was marching wearily towards the camp when they encountered two people in military uniform who turned out to be the manager of the mine, engineer-captain of the MVD by the name of Mulyar, a handsome gypsy-looking man, accompanied by the chief engineer. Mulyar affably greeted the throng and asked:

"Well, how is work? Any complaints?"

"Of course, citizen manager! All we get to eat is oats—morning, noon and night. This is intolerable– we are not horses! Why not change the cereal? Also, we don't get any tobacco..."

The swarthy boss smiled benevolently showing off his white teeth.

"Oats? But they are very good for you! Look at the chief engineer! Alexander Alexandrovich always eats an oatmeal porridge for breakfast and is a fine specimen of humanity! See how tall he is?

The nearly two meter tall chief engineer stood on his long legs and smiled happily. "On your way!"—he instructed the leader of the convoy, and that was the end of the grievance session.

Many prisoners kept in touch with home and some received letters and parcels, but these concessions did not extend to the émigrés. We had no news from home and could not send any messages either. It seemed that we existed in some kind of a shell, which did not allow us to hear or see anything. I knew that my father and younger brother Yuri were imprisoned somewhere, as was my cousin Tatiana, whom I unsuccessfully tried to meet when I was sent from the Diomid Bay to collect some foodstuffs from the Vladivostok prison. Life was going on in all its splendour somewhere else, whereas here all we had here were infinitely long winters, short summers and daily backbreaking slave labour.

The camp is a dreadful place for everybody except the professional criminals who get released, only to come back for another stint. Jail is their way of life. I also think that even though imprisonment is hard on everybody, those who know that they have committed a serious crime, such as murder, burglary or a major swindle, realise that they deserve to be punished, and that makes their sufferings morally justifiable. However, I had committed no crime and lived an exemplary life of a normal human being. I worked and tried to help others, only to be declared an "enemy of the people', for no reason at all and contrary to normal logic. That was a state of affairs, which I could not accept. My spirit was crushed by the realisation that I was a victim of crass injustice. Why? What have I done to deserve this nightmare?

White liners cross faraway seas, planes fly in the air, fast trains and cars cross continents; delightful music is being played and happy suntanned and good looking men and women lay on hot sands, sing, dance and fall in love. Waterfalls make a delightful noise in the mountains of my beloved Korea, the crowns of its trees swing in a free wind, the flowers are in bloom...And here all we see are barren rocky hills, the boggy tundra and low shrubs, barely reaching to my knees...

The time will come when I'll get to like Chukotka and will even miss it. But that was all in the future, whereas my surroundings were sheer hell during the years of my slavery. Thankfully, though, time did not stand still. The dates of our release were being posted on the notice boards. Our work detachment kept exceeding the production quota by 121% and certain sums of money were being added to my savings account. I was due to be released in 1954 now, and not, as previously, in 1957. If things continued as they had been, I could be out at end of summer of 1952. ..

CHAPTER 7

I was about to retire for the night when a slightly built prisoner, the orderly of our camp commandant, raced into the hut and blurted out:

"On the double to see the captain! He said to hurry..."

What the hell did he need me for? As far as I can recall, it was the first, and last, summons to the "boss". I quickly got dressed and repaired to the office next door to the guards' quarters, entered the room and made the customary announcement:

"As requested by you, prisoner...etc, etc..."

The captain sat in his cosy well-lit little office at a table covered with files. He looked through one of them, took out a photograph, and put it on the table.

"Sit down. Have a good look. Do you know this man?"

It took me a while to recognise my cousin Vasilii (*Basil)* Powers in the photograph of a man with a hunted expression on his face dressed in worn sailor's striped vest. Vasilii was the son of my long departed Aunt Lisa, nicknamed Tika, and I last saw him in Shanghai in the spring of 1941. I could not believe my eyes...

"Well, do you recognise him?"

"Yes. This is my cousin Vasilii Powers. But he has been living in Shanghai for a long time.. "

"He came here as a Japanese spy."

"A spy? I doubt it. He came with us (*from Vladivostok in the 1920's MH)* to Korea and then went to live in Shanghai. He is married and worked at a dogs' racecourse."

"What's that?"

"Well, dog races. He worked there as administrator and dog trainer. I heard that during the Japanese occupation of Shanghai he was arrested by their Gendarmerie *(equivalent of the KGB MH)* on suspicion of being a Russian agent. I also heard that he was severely beaten, but they eventually let him go."

"Correct. They beat him, recruited him to spy for them and sent your cousin here under the guise of a patriot returning home. However, he won't get away with that ruse here!"

I myself was once arrested and questioned at gunpoint in Manchuria by the Japanese Gendarmerie, also, by the way, on suspicion of being a potential Russian spy. The only reason for that was that I had the stupidity to examine some of their military vehicles at a railway station. I always thought that the Japanese were the most paranoid nation in the world, but was absolutely wrong. My compatriots turned out to be infinitely more suspicious, seeing a spy, a traitor and "an enemy of the people" in everybody. That trait seems to have become entrenched from the days of Stalin's terror, because before that it was inimical to the Russian nature.

That was the end of the questioning, but my testimony was most unlikely to have helped my unfortunate cousin, who, as I was to find out very much later, divorced his wife because she refused to return to Russia in 1947. That was the time when, in a macabre twist of irony, a huge number of Russian émigrés sailed to the Russian port of Nakhodka in ships called "Gogol" and "Dostoyevsky" *(famous Russian authors of the 19th century MH)*. Their quixotic journey gave rise to a sad joke popular at the time: "Dostoyevsky's 'Idiots' and Gogol's 'Dead Souls' have arrived home"... (*"Idiots" and "Dead Souls" are the names of Dostoyevsky's and Gogol's novels respectively MH.*)

Many years later, when I began writing articles in various magazines, I started to receive letters from people who, like I, went through the Gulag, but I had not heard a word about my cousins Vasilii and Phillip Powers. Both of them had been arrested in accordance with the notorious Article 58 of the penal code, although their circumstances were different. I fear that both of them were murdered by the system.

I learned in spring 1952 that Kvasov and Kalugin had been released and lived in Pevek. Soon after that I realised that, due to remissions, my imprisonment was going to end in July or August of that year. It was the time when model workers were being paid 400 roubles a month and I started to acquire a few items of personal wardrobe. I ordered a sporty suit made of cheviot (Rough woolen twill) cloth in the camp shop, acquired new kersey(ribbed woolen cloth) knee-high boots and ordered a cap. I also started to avoid the compulsory periodic hair clipping.

The wait for my release during the months immediately preceding it was frightening and exhausting. One heard that some released prisoners became institutionalised and asked to return to jail. That was akin to a blind man refusing a sight-restoring surgery because he was used to being looked after by others...

All those who were due for release had been photographed and lists of their names were posted on notice boards. And my name was on one of them, and at long last we were being taken to Pevek for an official release.

I said goodbye to my friends and scrambled aboard a truck, which already contained six prisoners and two armed guards, and off we went.

It was an unusually warm day as far as Chukotka was concerned, on which I was travelling along a road, which I regarded in 1948 as a path of no return.

Here again was the town of Pevek, Chukotka's northern gates. I saw its greyish- purple bay and a small settlement with a wharf, which was big enough to accommodate ocean-going liners. A few new two and three-storied homes appeared in the settlement as well as some barracks, huts and temporary structures. A few conical mud huts looking like "yarangs" *(transportable houses of the native inhabitants of the Arctic MH)* completed the scenery. It seemed that their purpose was to help the native inhabitants of Chukotka, the Chukcha people, to get used to a settled *(as opposed to nomadic MH)* way of life. A lagoon was located to one side of the bay. A lake occupied the middle of the settlement and round barren hills lay behind it. The prison camp was behind the settlement. It was a transit camp, which held prisoners who were due for release.

Inmates from all points of the Chaun-Chukotsk area of "Dalstroy" were assembled here, all of whom were awaiting their fate. New faces appeared every day and almost daily some of them were taken away. Was it to freedom or for an additional stretch behind bars? In any event, none of them ever came back. The situation was intolerable. I spent almost seven years in prison and saw and suffered all sorts of things. Life was also difficult in the "Krasnoarmeysky" camp, but I knew then that release was imminent, whereas time stood still here... One, two, three weeks had passed. All sorts of thoughts were going through my head, strengthened by various stories: "They'll call you and say:'you have to face a special tribunal'" Or another gem: "A special session of the court has decided to give everybody another five years." No wonder that I could hardly sleep during the three weeks on Pevek...

Finally, on the 13ᵗʰ of August 1952 a list was read out of those who had to go to the guardhouse and about ten of us reported to its gate. But where were the guards? To our great surprise a skinny civilian, some sort of a social worker, appeared at the gate instead if the guard and we followed him as a disorganised mob. He led us to the centre of the settlement and showed us a door with some sort of official signboard. I could not quite understand what it said. I seem to recall that it consisted of letters, which read something like: "USVITL CCGPU" *(a collection of nonsense syllables MH)*. Our social worker waved his hand:

"Go in and goodbye. You are on your own now. Come on, lads!"

We entered a hallway and sat on benches, which were standing around. Individual names were called out, with mine being also called at long last. I entered the room and stood in front of a man wearing a military uniform who beckoned to me. What will he announce? I waited with baited breath while the fellow was rummaging through the paper work. Here it was—he finally found my paper! He again looked me over and compared my face with the image on a small photograph, no bigger than a small postcard, which he put on the table in front of him.

"Here is your release form. Read it and sign this book."

YOU at last, and not the humiliating "thou"! I don't remember what I had to sign in the book, but I think that it had something to do with a non-disclosure of the goings-on in the camp. The next paper he handed to me was an official document, which was to accompany me during my life as a free citizen. It read in bold print : **CERTIFICATE OF RELEASE,** followed, in small print: "This is not an internal passport and cannot be used for a propiska *(a means of registering at a place of abode MH).* The left corner of that document contained a frightening photo of me with a shaven head. The document also contained my surname, date and year of birth, the place of birth and nationality, plus the fact that I was a stateless person. Last but not least, there was a signature and date: 4th of August 1952. The last bit was strange, as it seemed that I had been already free for nine days. Well, the bosses were obviously in no hurry, as it made no difference to them,

"What next?"

"Go to the Accounts Department and collect your cash" -growls the boss. "It's further down the corridor."

I was aware that I was getting a wage since 1949, but had no idea how much money could have accumulated in three years. Rumour had it that production workers received a decent wage, but there were deductions for everything: for food, clothing, the yearly Government

Loan and—very touching indeed—for our guards, without whom we most assuredly could not have survived!..

I was, nevertheless, pleasantly surprised at the sum I received from the Accounts: I was given ten thousand and six hundred roubles. It was a truly magnificent sum for an ex-prisoner.

I picked up a copy of the paper called "The Soviet Kolyma", which was lying around, wrapped my fortune in it and went outside. There was not a soul attached to my person! There was nobody to greet or farewell me, nobody to guard or boss me around. I asked a passer by the road to a savings bank and opened an account in which I deposited ten thousand roubles, leaving three 200 rouble notes for current expenses. I left the bank, not knowing what to do next until I remembered that my mate, the Old Believer Pyotr Kalugin, was renting a part of a room near the bay and was working as a labourer in the local shop.

Pevek was certainly no Paris or even Kiev, but following an old Russian saying: "the use of your tongue can take you as far as Kiev", I asked a few people and I finished up in the eastern outskirts of Pevek, on the shores of the bay, which looked dark blue on that day. Blue-white ice-floes, looking like a flock of swans, were drifting on its surface a fair distance away from the shore. A few clay shacks stood on the pebble-strewn shore about thirty metres away from the sea. I approached the one nearest to me and knocked.

"Come in!"

I opened the door and immediately recognised Kalugin whose beard was as magnificent as ever but was beginning to show a few grey streaks. He walked towards me stretched out his huge paw and hooted a double bass:

"Hello there! Come in! Fellows, this is one of ours—from over there... Let me introduce you. Let's have a drink to freedom, brother. We are just about to have lunch."

A few men sat around a roughly made table. A newspaper lay on the table and on top of it were huge slices of black bread and a few open tins of canned beef. They were accompanied by a pot of pure alcohol and a saucepan filled with water. Well-worn aluminium and enamelled mugs completed the décor. One could pour a required quantity of liquor and dilute it with water to taste.

We drank the first mug to freedom and the second one to the newly acquired friends. Petro Kalugin downed the second mug, stroked his beard and said to me:

"I told the lads that it is warm today and we should go for a swim but they don't believe and are making fun of my suggestion. Let's show them up, eh? Let's go!"

I was sure that it was a joke and immediately got up:

"Yes, let's!"

We left the shack and repaired for the seashore. Pyotr sat down on the pebbly beach, took off his boots, and I followed suit. The sun was warm all right, but the water...I knew that the water temperature in the Arctic Ocean never exceeds 6 to 8 degrees, even in summer. However, I was hoping that the performance was about to resolve itself in a joke and continued to undress. Pyotr got up and bravely walked into the water, stopping only when it reached above his knees. I followed, albeit reluctantly. My mate turned around and splashed me from head to toe with well-aimed handfuls of water. I responded in kind and the two of us rushed into the sea. The water scalded me, but I started swimming overarm and managed to cover a small circle, after which I raced out onto the pebbles like a scorched cat. Kalugin joined me and the rest of the group greeted our performance with a thunderous "hurrah!" Our white skins turned crimson red, but we rubbed ourselves down, got quickly dressed and raced back to the table to take another swig of a stiff drink.

My new friends worked as wharf labourers and had to start their shift after lunch, but I was keen to find Pyotr Xenofonovich Kvasov who was working somewhere as a head storeman. Kalugin told me that the stores were located in a settlement situated on the seventh kilometre of the Pevek-Valkumei Highway. The shortest way was to walk around the prison camp, and then to walk west away from Pevek, following a hillside overlooking the sea. We agreed to meet at a later date, and I was on my way.

It was four in the afternoon and the weather was truly magnificent, which was not surprising for Chukotka at that time of the year. It was the first time in seven years that I was walking as a free man. It is difficult to describe my feelings. Freedom again! I was walking cross country through tall wilting grass, followed by a field of cut hay, which ran along the hillside and finished up in the bay. The bay led to the Ocean, and it must have extended all the way to the North Pole. The feeling of freedom was quite overwhelming. These are the moments during which one fully comprehends the meaning of the word "happiness"!

The freshly cut hay exuded a sweet aroma and I approached small toy-like haystacks. It was a touching sight. It was obvious that large haystacks were not for the Arctic! How could they grow in this climate?

Oh God! What incredible beauty! I took a few steps and collapsed on one of the haystacks. Is it true or is it a dream? Yes, it is true, and no matter what happens tomorrow, today I am free and am lying on real hay and above me is a an incredibly dark blue sky!

I was lying down enjoying the feeling of freedom and realising that I was only three kilometres away from my target. Xenofontych and I will decide how to live next. I am certain to find all my nearest and dearest within at most a year, two or three. I'll see my wife, embrace my little son! How old is he by now? Six? Seven?..

And all of a sudden—voices. I raised my head and froze. A detachment of soldiers led by a sergeant was heading in my direction. I collapsed on the hay and lay still. "That's it. They've changed their mind. They have decided that my release was a mistake and are going to take me back to the Gulag, back behind the barbed wire". It was the second time within these few years when I would say: "The fairytale is over." No, it is better to die. I have no strength left to go through all that again!

Why should I look at these people during these last moments of freedom? I lay back looking at the sky; the detachment was getting ever closer and I could hear their voices...

Then all of a sudden—they walked past!

I did not move, did not blink and the voices started growing fainter. Where were they going and why?

That is, of course, beside the point. The point was that Fate quite unexpectedly had sent me a terrifying ordeal, which, I think, could have ended in a heart attack.

I lay motionless and took a fairly long time to come to. It was getting dark when I got to the stores and saw Pyotr Xenofontovich standing at the entrance to his abode.

"Valery! Sonny!"—said he stroking his beard.

We walked towards each other and embraced. Kvasov was eleven years older than me. He was already fifty two and I was "only" forty one, and my friend said that I was still quite young.

He was right, I suppose, but I felt that I had already lived two lifetimes...

The End

And a new beginning...

Please visit www.RussiansInKorea.com for more information about Valery Yankovsky and his life.

Postscript

Josef Stalin, Master of Terror

Joseph Stalin is gone now, but he is ranked in the top 15 "Most EVIL Dictators In History", a book of that name by Shelley Klein, published by Barnes&Noble.

Joseph Stalin killed more people than even Hitler managed to kill.

He was possibly the most successful dictator of Russia, yet he was not himself Russian, and his real name was not Stalin, but Iosif Vissarionovich Dzhugasvili, a Georgian. He chose "Stalin", because it means "man of steel" in Russian.

He was born in Georgia, south of Russia, a small country always dominated by the huge "Russian bear" just to the north of it.

Under his despotic rule, millions of Russians died in the GULAG labor camps, in prisons, or simply of starvation.

He abandoned his own son to die in a Nazi concentration camp, apparently refusing to negotiate for his release.

Did he perhaps see his rise to power as a perfect opportunity to exact revenge for his little country against the seemingly all-powerful Russians? Did he perhaps personify Georgia's vengeance against her overbearing neighbour?

We will never know, but he remains a hero in his home country.

He is gone now, but his spirit lives on in many countries around the world – North Korea, China, Cambodia, Sudan and other African locales, and just recently in Saddam's Iraq.

Joseph Stalin was a true anti-social personality, and his story illustrates how dangerous and destructive such a person can be.